Told in Toberona

John Swift

Watchword

Published by
Watchword
146 Sundrive Road, Dublin 12
email: watchwordinfo@gmail.com

June 2008

ISBN 978-0-9557249-1-6

Layout and Printing by
CRM Design + Print Ltd.
Dublin 12.

Typeset in 10pt Galliard
Produced by trade union labour in Ireland

Permission to reproduce copyright material is gratefully acknowledged.
Every effort has been made to trace copyright holders but if any have been inadvertently overlooked
the necessary arrangements will be made at the first opportunity.

Contents

Foreword

This memoir by John Swift (1896-1990) was in gestation for almost three quarters of a century, the first draft of his Dundalk childhood having been written on the Western Front during World War 1. Subsequently, throughout his life, he would periodically devote months of his free time to writing about his early life, particularly his childhood in Dundalk, his imprisonment as a conscientious objector during the First World War and his experiences in that war, only to abandon the writing when distracted by some other activity. This pattern prevailed into his nineties.

Convinced from an early age that my father's experiences were worth recording, I assumed he would eventually write a memoir. But, by 1985, when he was 89 years of age and his health was clearly deteriorating, it finally occurred to me that he might never undertake this task. I, therefore, asked him if he would have any objections to me writing his biography. Although he was immediately amenable to this proposal, his conception of the book I would write differed from mine, being confined mainly to his trade union career and, consequently, excluding his childhood, his imprisonment and his war experiences, important elements, in my view, in his formative years and essential material for the rounded, chronological biography I had envisaged. Aside from his early experiences and his later involvement in the labour movement, it was my intention to cover his active participation in a wide range of cultural, historical and other societies, several of which he had co-founded.

While our different conceptions of that project were neither discussed nor resolved, I proceeded to write the book I had in mind, with his wholehearted support and co-operation. However, when I was approaching the conclusion of my manuscript, he declared: 'I'll write my own book'. Elaborating on this some months later, in an interview with the *Irish Times* (*An Irishman's Diary*), published on 1 October 1988, he said: 'I can approach it from a more intimate standpoint'. Given his previous tendency to commence and later abandon such an undertaking, and his indifferent health at that time, I thought it unlikely that this project would ever see the light of day. I was wrong! In February 1989, at the age of 92, he finally produced his memoir, *Told in Toberona – One Man's Labour History*.

My own biography of him, *John Swift: An Irish Dissident*, was published in May 1991, some 14 months following his death. For several reasons, publication of his memoir was problematic, not least because it was a second book on essentially the same subject at roughly the same time. It was, therefore, decided to let the matter rest for a considerable period.

Efforts to secure a publisher were underway in 2007 when I accepted an invitation to participate in a new, 'not-for profit' publishing body, Watchword, whose principal object is the publication of labour related material which might not otherwise be published. Watchword subsequently decided to publish my father's manuscript.

One of the very few written accounts of the experiences of an Irishman during the First World War, Swift's memoir is possibly the only account of an Irish conscientious objector in that momentous event. It is also one of the very few autobiographical accounts by an 'ordinary' person of that era.

I wish to acknowledge the contribution of the late Catherine McDonnell who typed the original manuscript.

I wish to thank the following for their assistance with the publication of this book: the staffs of the National Library of Ireland and the Public Library, Dundalk, Co. Louth; my Watchword colleagues for their decision to publish the manuscript; Charles Callan, Liz Murray, David Swift and Justin Swift for proof reading; David Swift for photo editing; and Justin Swift for converting the typewritten version into electronic format and producing the musical notation in the final chapter.

For his determination and efforts to bring this publication to fruition, I am grateful to Fergus White. Special thanks are due to Charles Callan for, not only designing the cover and compiling the index, but being centrally involved in virtually every aspect of the project.

Finally, for their support and encouragement in securing publication of the manuscript, I would like to thank my sister and brother, Alice Robinson and (Patrick) Grosvenor Swift; my wife, Adrienne, and our sons, David, Justin, John, Neville and Robert.

John P. Swift

14 Clonard Grove
Dundrum
Dublin 16
E-mail: johnpswift@eircom.net
Telephone: 01-2958787

June 2008

List of Illustrations

Four Provinces House mural 1946, by Frances Kelly, depicting the Lord Mayor fulfilling his duty to check the weight of bread in the market, bread being sold by weight in earlier times.

Four Provinces House mural 1946, by Nano Reid, depicting procession of the Dublin Trades' Guilds, with the bakers' banner on the right.

Four Provinces House mural 1946, by Nano Reid, depicting the co-operative experiment at Ralahine, Co. Clare, 1831-1833.

Four Provinces House mural 1946, by Nano Reid, depicting James Connolly organising the Belfast Branch of the ITGWU in 1911.

John Swift speaking at a social function in the Four Provinces House Library in the late 1940s.

Four Provinces House Library - form of volume of 'The Complete Plays of Bernard Shaw', signed by the author, 9 October 1947.

John Swift, aged approximately 58, c. 1954.

John Swift, aged 60, Dublin, 27 April 1957.

The Swift family, from left: (Patrick) Grosvenor, Harriet, John, Alice and John, Dublin, 16 July 1960.

Harriet Swift (née Hendy) (1911-1990) and John Swift, aged 70, Dublin, August 1966.

John Swift, aged approximately 68, and Harriet Swift, guests at a trade union convention in the USA, mid-1960s.

John Swift, aged 77, at the Inaugural General Meeting of the Irish Labour History Society, Newman House, St. Stephen's Green, Dublin, on 27 October 1973.

Flanked by, from left, Ruairi Quinn, TD, Deputy Leader, and Dick Spring, TD, Leader of the Labour Party, John Swift, aged 93, at a Labour Party social function in his honour, in Dáil Éireann, Dublin, on 6 December 1989.

Back cover

John Swift, aged 70, Dublin, early 1967.

Chapter 1

Shortly after the founding of the Irish Labour History Society in October 1973 I was asked by the editor of the *Education Times*, John Horgan, to write an article on what the Society was about, for the *Education Times*, a well edited periodical published by the *Irish Times*. Perhaps the number of weeks it survived before closing for want of readership may be taken as an index of our country's interest in or concern for education. Our country could sustain periodicals on horse-racing, football and pop music, but not on education.

In the article I tried to keep to the shallows rather than wandering into the still modest depths my readings may have attained in the subject of Labour History. With such approach I ventured the definition that Labour History was the account of people at work and, more particularly, of their efforts to determine the conditions of their work. Later I felt somewhat flattered in reading a report of my definition being quoted, apparently with acceptance, by a no less notable and informed authority in the Irish Labour movement than Donal Nevin, General Secretary of the Irish Congress of Trade Unions.

Yet I was not satisfied with the definition, feeling the roots sprung from deeper levels. But, then, much of our definition is accepted not for theoretical but rather for practical ends, and thus deemed satisfactory. Reflecting on these matters I remember readings in Hegel, that profound thinker whose work inspired what we know as Marxian dialectics. Hegel taught that all determination (definition) is negation. When we determine what a thing is we also determine what it is not.

I have no desire to encumber what I am writing here with anything like the logical dialectics of either Hegel or Marx. But I have been conscious that the definition I gave of Labour History in the *Education Times*, though having the virtue of brevity, could be somewhat arbitrary and restrictive. Perhaps it was my early, some would say, too early, introduction to studies in what was then called political economy and in what I came to regard as related sciences that suggested a much broader definition to be given Labour History.

I was at an age when my formal education was, and from its start had been, under the guidance of ecclesiastical authority. First, I was a pupil in what was called the Grande School, a kindergarten run by the Sisters of Mercy in their Dundalk Convent. The kindergarten had both male and female pupils. When the boys came to seven years of age they had to leave, to continue their education elsewhere. The girl pupils could remain on, to finish their education in the higher classes in the convent school where the educational aim was to turn out well-mannered young ladies, with no capability of earning a living, the like not being apprehended by an education that saw its pupils as above such necessity. The pupils were destined for more gracious living by the grace of holy and successful matrimony. In those days but few females of the petty and higher bourgeois classes demeaned themselves with work.

When my term in the kindergarten ended I began in the secondary school of the Irish Christian Brothers in Dundalk. There was also in the town a national school for boys that catered for the less well-off classes. This was run by the De La Salle Order of Christian Brothers. The pupils of each of these schools of Christian Brothers kept much to themselves as a class, and the Brothers in each did little or nothing to promote anything like brotherhood between the pupils of both.

In the nuns' kindergarten and in both Christian Brothers' schools the chief aim of the education was to produce pupils who would be worthy of being known as good citizens of a country traditionally known as the Island of Saints and Scholars. About this so often boasted heritage I already had doubts, hearing my father comment that the vaunted scholarship was all about the saints and the saints themselves a poor lot as saints go or rather went, as we're here considering ages past - their calibre and achievements hardly meriting the attention of serious scholarship. Making comparisons he would cite some of the first-raters such as Augustine, Aquinas, Francis of Assisi, the Great Gregory.

From my early years with the Brothers my father showed much interest in my schooling. He had schooled himself, mostly with popular books of science in many of its branches. He had several books about the sun, the planets and stars, and took pains that his talks about these at home should shed some light on my school education. To counter the cosmology of the Book of Genesis being taught me by the Brothers, he would talk of the discoveries of Copernicus and Galileo and other scientists.

My father took the evident attention I paid his talks on astronomy as a sign of my interest in scientific subjects generally. Presuming on that he started me on readings in Darwin's *Origin of Species*. This introduction to the biological sciences he planned as prologue to further studies I was to undertake in the social sciences, including economics. I was soon to learn from readings in Darwin that all living creatures, including human beings, could exist or persist only to the degree of their using their organs or faculties. Thus it seemed the human activities in which I was later to be interested from readings in economics and labour history were biological in origin. I was to be conscious of that particular thought in all my subsequent readings in the social sciences.

Meanwhile, in my early days under the Christian Brothers I was well launched in economic life, engaged in activities not without relevance for the student of economics and labour history, and indeed of the other important social science, ethics. I was in the thick of our school's black-market. Many of the pupils were the sons of business people with shops and stores. In our school market we bartered in varied merchandise, including sweets, toys, cakes, cigarettes. In most cases the goods the pupils brought to the market were stolen from their parents' stocks. With my contribution of cakes I was in a strong position in the market.

Some of the young enter their trade or profession by dint of their fitness, or through strong personal initiative, or yet through the influence of others. I entered mine by stealth, or rather literally by stealing. I suppose it was not an unusual mode of entry to, and, more positively, progress in, the great world of trade and commerce. On one of my forays to replenish stock I was caught by the foreman. He was making an unexpected after-work visit to the bakehouse, on some mission, perhaps as illicit as the one that brought me there.

I was now in dread he would report me to my father. He chose rather to blackmail me, offering me immunity if I agreed to do some services for him. The services started in doing errands for him, running out to buy his cigarettes, or to deposit slips and money at the bookies, or yet to deliver sealed notes to his current sweetheart then in service to a family in the quality residential part of the town. These commissions grew to performing little jobs in the bakehouse, work I found more satisfying since it gave me the feeling I was now earning my daily replenishments of cake stocks. These were now being secured with not only the knowledge but the good-will and co-operation of the foreman.

As for my father, when he learned I was spending some of my after-school time doing jobs in the confectionery bakehouse, he also felt satisfaction that his trade and that of his ancestors had now prospects of being carried on to future generations. I found the work in the bakehouse the more rewarding in the feeling of acquiring new skills and in the exercise itself of those physical as well as mental faculties which, from the readings in Darwin, nature had given her creatures, for use in the ordained way of earning their living.

Indeed, I was now so interested in becoming a competent confectioner that I longed more and more for escape from the boring readings, thrust on me by my father. But escape was not to be. I had still to do my readings in biology and sociology. These usually followed or accompanied my school homework, when my father would interrogate me on the day's schooling and table his corrections or amendments.

As for the evening readings I thought there could be few books so forbidding for the young reader as the two that came out all but simultaneously around mid-nineteenth century, Darwin' s *Origin of Species* and Marx's *Capital*, works destined to be revolutionary in so broad a field of human thought.

In the evening readings prescribed by my father I complained of the tedium that brings incomprehension. In Darwin I tried to learn something of the structure and habits of innumerable organisms from earthworms to mammoth creatures now long extinct. Thinking to make my readings less unendurable my father would quote the saying attributed to Dr. Johnson that genius is an infinite art of taking pains. With the authors of *The Origin of Species* and *Capital* in mind I thought to add the addendum that genius was an infinite art of taking pains - and passing the pains on to others.

I continued my after-school work in the bakehouse up to my quitting school. I was then fifteen years of age. It was my mother who brought this turn in events. She was far from satisfied with my entering the ancestral trade. Her ambitions for me rose to the professions. Through the influence of her first cousin, head law-clerk in the principal law firm in the town, she worked to get me started there. This was the firm of Moynagh's. It was headed by Dr.

Michael C. Moynagh, a graduate of Trinity College, Dublin. He was Crown Solicitor for the County Louth, and for some reason which I never heard explained he had been made a recipient of the French Legion of Honour. He had two sons in the firm, Frank, a barrister, and Stephen, a solicitor.

I started in Moynagh's as a junior clerk, and my wages were a half-crown a week. The further arrangement was, according to my mother and her cousin, if after a period I liked the work and the firm liked me I would be apprenticed to become a solicitor. My work was mostly in copying deeds and affidavits and other legal documents. I found the work, unlike that in the bakery, very leisurely. We had time even to browse in the big leather-bound law books on the office shelves. I suppose it was this that led to our office games at definition, an art coming well within the compass of legal training.

Finding perusal of the law volumes even more boring than my early readings in Darwin and Marx, I made a play in our definition games which said that genius is an infinite art of taking pains and passing the pains on to others. A senior clerk with much more experience in matters legal than I thought my definition did not explain enough, and ventured the amendment that genius was an infinite art in taking pains and, in the case of authors lacking literary flair, passing the pains on to their readers. I objected to this, claiming that brevity being the soul of wit, over-loading the wit with explanations tends to smother the soul. Then the question occurred to me, whose wit and whose soul? The lawyer's wit, especially when committed to brief, will certainly not be in brevity but rather in verbosity; his soul, in the mileage of the marathon, its extent to be calculated by his running-mate, the costings-clerk.

The sedentary character of the law work was beginning to bore me. The fact that it did not involve my physical faculties in the production of a thing palpable seemed to me an unsatisfying activity. I renewed my association with some former school-mates and we started a physical culture club in an unoccupied old house in one of the back streets. There we indulged in vigorous exercises, in boxing, wrestling and weight-lifting. In school we had been encouraged to play cricket and football, but I had not taken to those games, or to field athletics.

I was aware, too, that my father was unhappy with my working in Moynagh's firm. The head of the firm being Crown Solicitor had to handle briefs on behalf of his Majesty's Government, and this meant having to prosecute in political as well as civil cases. My father was a strong Nationalist; and in the town there were still rumblings of Fenianism and a few of the towns-people had recently started a branch of Sinn Féin. He would have been greatly embarrassed had it happened that the local newspaper reported Dr. Michael Moynagh's appearances in the local court, prosecuting someone for political felony.

But the Crown Solicitor was now very old, and had all but ceased appearing in Court. The short walk from the offices in Roden Place to the Courthouse had become too much for his aching limbs. His walks indeed had become short, if frequent. In his pacing from his private office to make circuit of the general office, he would pause at the different desks, when he would hail the occupant with some quote of precedent, sometimes from the law book, its point or meaning depending on the particular case engaging the clerk at the desk. The doctor would talk loud on these rounds, so that the rest of us clerks at our desks should hear him and thus become educated in the law. On these occasions there was usually respectful silence in the place, but sometimes broken by the rat-tat from an inner office. It was the clatter of the new machine, the typewriter, and some of us junior clerks, must have imagined its barrage as that of a machine gun, not the least of whose targets would be the hand-writing exercises then holding an important place in the Brothers' classes and now apparently made superfluous by the new technology. Some of our pens were now working more carefully and diligently on the parchments.

Around the time we started our physical culture club my father was having more serious worries about the law than any fears he had of my employer, Dr. Moynagh, being involved in political prosecutions. Our bakery was now on the point of bankruptcy; and the dreaded day soon came when big notices appeared on the street hoardings announcing the bankrupt sale of bakery premises with delivery vans and horses and other effects.

Thus ended my brief involvement at the fringes of the legal profession. Perhaps it had its uses when later I came to work in preparing and handling briefs in another sphere of case-making and advocacy, that which we call collective bargaining.

I suppose my father was too much of an idealist to survive in business in the commercial ruthlessness developing in this town midway between the cities of Dublin and Belfast. The now partly mechanised bakeries in both cities, with the new rail facilities, were able to deliver bread in Dundalk to be sold at prices much lower than those being charged by the local firms.

My father was an old-fashioned craftsman, a Luddite adverse to machinery in the trade. Against mechanisation in the bakery he could make scientific argument that the metal manipulation in dough-mixing machines and in metal scalers and moulders pounded the natural flavour elements out of the dough, resulting in tasteless bread.

Many of us will be inclined to agree with that, when we recall the nutty flavour of the old handmade crusty loaf and turnover, and compare them with the modern mass-produced sliced and wrapped bread, which for tastelessness someone has likened it to blotting paper. My father would insist the making of good bread was necessarily a slow and nursing process from the start of fermentation through the proofing and moulding stages on to the not less meticulous process, the baking.

After the failure of our bakery we were soon to learn more about the less leisurely processes of the trade in the metropolis. Like many before us failing in trade in the provinces, our family made for Dublin. There we settled in a tenement in a slum area. My father found casual work, in one bakery today, and, if lucky, in another the next, and in each working with machines that had put him and others that had been tied to handcraftsmanship out of business.

I found work at the trade as an improver. It was in the confectionery department of Galbraith's bakery in the Dublin Liberties. The confectionery side of the trade was not yet seriously affected by machinery. Back at the more urgent modes of the bakehouse, I could now forget about the Moynaghs, the

Doctor's quotes, the encroachments of the typing clatter, the concern of both about precedents, some of them famous in the law books. I could now harken to things more simple, more elemental, but with their own subtlety, the stir of the brooding yeast, the changing breath of an oven, the tired yawn of its furnace, all constituents in the morning's work of adding graces to the commonplace, the lustre and taste of a bun.

This was in 1912, the year following the dispute in the trade in Dublin that shattered the bakery workers' union to make it impotent for a few years. In the 1911 dispute the Union had challenged the introduction of machinery in some of the larger Dublin bakeries. The challenge failed. The firms affected recruited non-union labour and in a few weeks got back into more or less normal business.

The weekly working hours at the trade at this time could be sixty hours or more, with no stated overtime. Night-baking was universal. After leaving Galbraith's bakery in Vicar Street I worked in the Ballsbridge bakery of Johnston, Mooney & O'Brien. Usually confectionery was manufactured in the day, often in the same premises as bread was made at night. In the Ballsbridge bakery the confectionery was made at night, in an underground cellar-like adjunct to the main bakehouse where the bread-making went on. The confectionery bakehouse had only one entrance, a narrow one down stone steps from the bread bakehouse. It had no windows or roof ventilation, so, with little regard at the time for work-safety and hygiene regulations, the smoke and sulphur from the old-fashioned ovens made working conditions most disagreeable, and, we feared, unhealthy. A few of us youngest of the hundred or more working in the Ballsbridge bakery started a physical culture club in an outhouse in Beechwood Avenue, Ranelagh. Apart from any enthusiasm we shared for physical exercise, we thought it an antidote that might rid our bodies of some of the poison matter inhaled and ingested in our nights in the bakehouse.

Shortly after I started work in the Ballsbridge bakery I became a member of the union. At the time, late 1915, only a few of the workers in this bakery, as in some of the other large bakeries in the city, were union members. I left the firm in 1916, just after the Rebellion, to take a job in Bewley's bakery in Westmoreland Street. I still had the status of improver. My wages were as before £1 a week, but it was day-work and the hours were shorter. I was the only worker in the firm a member of a trade union. I thought to do some organising among the bakery staff. My work was unavailing and late in 1916 was rewarded with dismissal by the bakery foreman.

At this time things were going badly for Britain in the First World War. It was in the aftermath of the disastrous Battle of the Somme and the intensified enemy submarine blockade. British policy in Ireland was then planned to run down industrial employment here with the object of recruiting the unemployed for service in the armed forces, or alternatively offering jobs in Britain, then available in plenty following the call-up of young British workers for military service under the Conscription Act of 1916. The slump of work here affected even the bakery trade, and some of us unemployed and signing up at the Labour Exchange were offered emigration or what was called commutation grants by our union. The young and single among the unemployed members were thus encouraged to leave so that the work available could be shared by the married members.

In the Labour Exchange there were agents of British firms recruiting for workers to take jobs in various parts of Britain. We were given to understand that refusal of work for which one would be thought capable would mean cutting off entitlement to unemployment benefit. It was in these circumstances twenty of us young and able-bodied unemployed were signed up for labouring work in a lead works in Rotherhithe, London. We arrived in London 1st June, 1917. We were housed in a lodging-house on Bow Road. The work, loading blast-furnaces and handling heavy ingots of lead, was physically exhausting. Production went on in shifts through the twenty-four hours in a seven-day working week. The heat and fumes of the furnaces made the work even more disagreeable than that endured in the old-fashioned bakehouses. The weekly wages were £2. The name of the firm was Einthoven.

What we felt worse in the job was the resentment of some of the permanent workers there. They had been exempted from military service, either through age or disability, and they resented our having been imported to take the jobs of their younger and able-bodied colleagues, some of them sons or other relatives, now conscripted in the armed forces. After a few weeks at the work we felt ourselves goaded into strike. This of course was highly illegal and prohibited by the Defence of the Realm Regulations. Myself and a colleague were singled out as ring-leaders and brought before a Tribunal. We pleaded our grievances in justification. They undertook to investigate them, but fined us £2 each and warned us that a repetition of the offence would bring withdrawal of our exemption from military service and our being handed over to the military authorities.

After a few weeks back at work we could see no sign of investigation of the conditions, which remained as before. Some of us struck again, and, anticipating that the ineffective action would soon bring the authorities on the job, we decided on escape from the lead works, to chance the hazard of going on the run in London. Of the few of us each went off on his own. After a few days I got another job as builder's labourer in the London suburb of Eltham. The work was at constructing aeroplane hangars. The war in the air was intensifying, and we had experienced raids on London. Contractors building hangars or at other work regarded as specially urgent by the authorities were paid bonuses for its quick completion. Labour was short and the contractors were ready to engage hands without asking awkward questions as to the workers' bona fides under the Military Service Act.

I was working there, assisting carpenters, only a few weeks when I was arrested by the Military Police. They were very active at this time, searching for deserters from the armed forces and absentees under the Military Service Acts. I came under the latter category. They had made an early morning raid on the lodging house where I was staying. This was the Rowton House Workmen's lodging in Lewisham. Similar in purpose to Dublin's Iveagh Hostel, there was a chain of these in Britain. They were founded by Baron Rowton who had been a director of Messrs Arthur Guinness & Company.

My subsequent adventures in the hands of the British Military Authorities have been recorded elsewhere. As this writing is intended as a brief account of my labour history I will try to keep what follows about my detention, court martial and prison experiences within that context. I had been brought to the Chelsea headquarters of the London Irish Rifles, and on refusing there to put on military uniform. I was escorted by the Military Police to Winchester. There, in the barracks of the Regiment's Field Training Headquarters, I was again ordered to undress and put on uniform. On refusing again I was brought before an officer and committed to detention to await court martial.

In this training headquarters the only labour I could see going on was that of the commissariat engaged in cooking, maintaining, doctoring and scavenging for the thousand or so men of the regiment. The regiment spent the days drilling in totally unproductive operations in fields made barren of growth by mass tramping and the assaults of war machines and their pollutants. Each day had its mass rituals of unproductiveness, the waste made solemn by absurd ceremony, with its acolytes, the officers' servants, occupied in polishing the buttons and brasses of their masters and pressing their masters' trousers to an edge matching that of their ceremonial swords. It saddened one to reflect on the waste of energy and material in training soldiers to kill or maim other soldiers, and perhaps other humans who were not soldiers. Part of the waste went in watching me in a cell and keeping me equally unproductive.

I was tried by court martial on charge of disobeying a lawful military command, found guilty and sentenced to two years imprisonment with hard labour. The first part of the sentence was to be served in Wormwood Scrubs prison in London, whither I was escorted by Military Police. As regards the hard labour part of my sentence, there was no labour to the solitary confinement I was to endure for four weeks in this prison, and the hardness was rather in the sloth sustained daily in walking up and down the narrow cell to the point of exhaustion, then, the cell furniture of table, stool and plank-bed having been removed in the morning, sitting or lying on the stone floor.

I was transferred from there to Wandsworth Jail. There I was permitted work in my cell. The work, or hard labour, was like to that of a shoe-maker, sewing pieces of leather on to mail-bags for His Majesty's postal service. There was irony in this in that for my several months' confinement in three prisons I was not permitted to receive or send out any mail. When Alfred Byrne, Member of the Irish Parliamentary Party for Dublin Harbour constituency at the time, enquired in the British House of Commons as to my whereabouts in the British prisons he was refused information.

Later I was permitted to do the sewing work in a work-room where other prisoners, including conscientious objectors and the ordinary civil prisoners, were gathered doing similar work. 'Gathered' could be a misleading term, as each prisoner was kept at such distance from the others by the over-seeing warders, it was difficult to sustain communication with any of them. Still, with whispers and signs, a certain amount of communication went on.

Any of the conscientious objectors I was able to engage in brief and whispered chats struck me as being rather solemn, churchy types, ready to quote scripture and hardly responsive or sympathetic to my particular objection to serving in the British armed forces. They were mostly pacifist Quakers, of public school education, their people of the middle and employing classes. This is not to criticise their stand against military service. Some of these objectors had been very roughly handled by their jailers, military and civil. There were cases among them of suicide and mental breakdown from suffering in captivity. Hearing of such cases at the time I thought I was getting off fairly well in not having so far encountered any attempt at physical violence to my person. This was leading me to presume that I being an Irishman my custodian had made certain allowances in my case and could hardly expect anything better. On the other hand, as regards the pacifist conscientious objectors, these were Britishers, and no allowances could be made for their refusal to fight for or defend Britain.

Still, from my furtive contacts with them I did not take much to the conscientious objectors. Perhaps this was a mixture of class bias and thinking them smug. At any rate, I felt more towards making the surreptitious contacts with the ordinary prisoners or criminals. I had made little progress here when an event occurred that was to bring me another change in habitation.

We were now in the second week in November, and still doing a few hours daily at the mail-bags in the work-room. One afternoon, through our whispering and gesture lines, we heard something about what was to become known as the Petrograd October Revolution according to the then Russian calendar, but which occurred at the end of the first week of November in our calendar. News of the Russian Revolution had reached us in a newspaper that one of the conscientious objectors had managed to have had smuggled in by a member of a visiting committee.

The news started much excitement among us, raising our hopes of a quicker end of the war and perhaps our earlier release. The rumours now circulating developed into something like a celebration of whistling and cat-calls. This was answered by the shouts and threats of the warders to keep order. When something like the normal silence was restored I was accused by one of the senior warders of leading the whistling. I had not whistled on the occasion but had shared in the jubilation.

It was on my record that when in solitary confinement in Wormwood Scrubs I had been charged before the deputy governor with persistent whistling in a manner likely to disturb the peace of the prison. In the silence of the Scrubs cell I had tried to make whatever sound I could by walking up and down on the stone flags and whistling loud. I was very fond of the Verdi operas, having learned by heart many of his martial tunes. I had been warned about the whistling by the elderly, but not unkind cockney warder, who was being kept on in service, owing to the call-up of the younger prison staff for military service.

But the whistling and loud marching had become something like compulsive with me. I had an irresistible need to make sound of some kind, if only to assure myself I was not in some soundless limbo or indeed in the grave itself. After many warnings, the warder booked me for an appearance before his superiors, when I was charged with breach of the prison regulations by loud whistling of rebel Irish songs! With severe warning, I was put on three days bread and water diet, which meant no great deprivation considering the current standard of the prison dietary. The result of this was of course to leave me even less fit to undertake any of the hard labour prescribed in my sentence.

It thus extended the period of my being without work, or in other words, lengthened the break in my labour history. And now, in Wandsworth, there was this sudden end to my work on the mailbags, and the charge again of whistling, this time in rejoicing at the Russian Revolution. I was escorted from the work-room to my cell and left there in confinement until the afternoon of the next day, when the cell door was opened and a military officer and two redcaps (military police) appeared, and I was commanded to accompany them. They escorted me along a series of corridors and stairways to what appeared to be a new extension of Wandsworth Prison, but what turned out to be a prison to itself, a military jail for the punishment of members of the armed forces convicted of military crimes.

When lodged in a cell the first thing I noticed was its coldness. Unlike the cell, serviced with moderate central heating, which I had been taken from, this one had no heat. This was a new penalty added to the jail hardships, and was not to be overcome by my vain efforts to sleep that night. Next day I was brought meals in my cell, the pattern being much the same as former Wandsworth dietary, the watery porridge, the few ounces of rough bread with a scrape of margarine, and a mug of weak liquid tasting like cocoa for breakfast, the almost meatless stew and dumpling at mid-day, and again the cocoa with another few ounces of bread, a scrape of margarine and a thin slice of cheese for supper.

What I wanted more was some information as to what they proposed doing with me, what labour, hard or otherwise, they intended assigning me and, more immediate, were they doing anything about the cold that was making me, chilled and somewhat feverish, almost immobile. That evening, after they served supper, in the usual way of opening aperture in door and handing in tray, an officer and two redcaps entered the cell. The redcaps carried military clothing, tunic, trousers, puttees, shirt, underclothes and boots. The officer brusquely ordered me to take off the prison garb and don the uniform. I replied I would not. At that the officer barked orders to the redcaps, whereon they dropped the uniform items to the floor and seized me. I was in no state to put up much of a resistance, and after a vain struggle they up-ended me and threw me to the floor, the back of my head hitting the flags. They then proceeded to pull and tear the prison clothes from me. This done they departed leaving behind on the floor the military clothing they had brought and taking with them my prison garb.

Left alone again in the cell I was now feeling quite ill. The shock and the soreness and numbness at the back of my head from the fall, along with feverishness from the cold, had brought on fits of coughing. But my worst feeling was of inner hurt and humiliation that I had not been able to resist or thwart them. But I was still determined not to put on the military clothes. It was now dark in the cell, save for a glimmer of lamp-light coming from a glass covered square in the wall over the cell door. The plank bed, table and stool had been removed from the cell that morning by the redcap warders. This followed the practice experienced when I was in solitary confinement in Wormwood Scrubs. Naked and desperate, I started to use the military clothes, some of them to make a pad to sit or stretch on in a corner of the cell and the remainder to cover parts of myself from the awful cold. I tried to settle down in some way but became aware of peeps from outside through the spy-hole in the cell door. These, like my other woes of coughing, the throbbing head pain, and the delirium when I attempted to doze, had now added to their assaults the ache of expectancy.

I don't know at what hour before or after midnight the door was opened when an officer with a redcap orderly appeared in the cell. The officer, who turned out to be a medical man, proceeded to examine me, taking my temperature and heart-beat. His stilted remarks sounded more like commands than enquiries about my condition. He had a few words with the orderly who had opened a medical case he had been carrying. After the two had busied themselves at the case they came forward and put me prostrate sideways on the floor, when the officer gave me an injection in the hip. He said brusquely it would soon make me warm.

I had begun feeling less conscious of the cold and the pain and was feeling the onset of drowsiness when, at the officer's order, the orderly left the cell. He returned shortly with another orderly, the two having brought a stretcher on wheels to the cell door. At the officer's orders they started to dress me in some of the clothes I had been using as a makeshift bed and covering. I had sunk into a state of stupor and had no clear notion of what they were doing. It was not till late in the morning when I slowly came to in the prison hospital that I discovered how the orderlies had dressed me for my hospital bed. They had clothed me in the coarse vest, the thick, dark grey shirt and khaki trousers of the British soldier. Too feeble to attempt removing them in the bed, I was still struggling with revulsion at the hated garments when an orderly arrived to divest me of them and clothe me in pyjamas of heavy, rough material. These, I supposed, were also of standard army pattern; but somehow they were not so offensive to me as the divested garments, particularly the khaki trousers. Besides, still feeling pain and fever, I had little choice in such matters.

Soon afterwards an officer appeared on the scene, the scene of this unusual hospital being the link-up together of some of the prison cells, with their partition walls largely remaining, but with a narrow passage providing communication between them. There were always orderlies on duty to see that the prisoner patients did not communicate with one another.

This officer now at my bed proved to be quite different to the one I had encountered in my previous cell. Both of them, I was to learn, were qualified doctors of the Royal Army Medical Corps. They wore the uniform and trappings of the army infantry officers. This medical man at once showed himself much less formal than the former one. Over the several days he was attending me I learned something about him. Perhaps he was the only person in the whole of Wandsworth prison, or prisons, who was happy at being there. The reason apparently was that Oscar Wilde had spent some of his prison term there. The medical officer told me of another Wilde association. Either he or his father, I'm not sure which, had been a pupil in Portora School, Enniskillen, Co. Fermanagh, where Wilde had received part of his education.

Up to that time in Wandsworth the name of Oscar Wilde had for me been a term of opprobrium. Any reference I had heard of him at home in Ireland had to do with his homosexuality, rather than with his literary or dramatic works. The emphasis on Wilde's pederasty had struck a sore note with me. In my younger days, when at school, I had been approached on a few occasions by adult men in attempts to have homosexual relations with me. My revulsion at the like was still strong, so much so, I was beginning to suspect and fear there was something of a homosexual about this officer-doctor's growing friendliness and, I thought, over familiarity with me. It had started with his recitals of some of Wilde's poetry and epigrams. Later he went on to quote passages of erotic prose which I took to be from Wilde but which, when I later came to read that author, I did not find in his works.

In efforts to get my doctor off his favourite subject I tried to divert his interest to other topics, including the urgent one of myself and my future in the prison. He responded with sympathy and offered advice. He spoke of the recent changes in the conscription law which had made it possible for conscientious objectors to undertake what was termed non-combatant service under the army authorities. Already many of the objectors had availed of service at ambulance or other medical work, and at other civilian activities, such as road making and maintenance, agricultural work and various trades.

I had heard something of this in the work-room in Wandsworth, and was aware some of the objectors I was able to communicate with there were interested and ready to take advantage of the change. And now this officer-doctor was strongly advising me to take advantage of it by offering to work under the military at my trade as a baker. There were many bakeries operating under the authorities. My first reaction to the idea was to dismiss it as an unacceptable compromise. But it was to become less objectionable when he pointed out the likely result of my continuing to refuse wearing the uniform. If I persisted in my attitude, on my return from the hospital to my unheated cell, in perhaps a week or less, there would be there no prison clothes but rather the army uniform for me to put on, if I were not again to suffer dangerous exposure. I could, of course, repeat what I did before, but how long could that go on?

He told me of cases within his own experiences when objectors persisting in their refusal to wear uniform and going through a repetition of the events I had just experienced, and ending up with death. I remembered now when I was awaiting court martial at Winchester and had for company in the guard-room cell a conscientious objector who was also awaiting trial. He was objecting to military service as a Tolstoyian anarchist. He had already served a term of imprisonment under the conscription legislation, and he was back again following further refusal to obey orders. I was surprised he was in army uniform, which he wore with obvious distaste and slovenliness. He thought it might be unwise for me to take a stand on the matter of the uniform. I should don the uniform, then refuse subsequent orders, say, commands, to go on parade, or handle arms. It appears that some of the early objectors had objected from the start by refusing, as I did, to put on the uniform and on being committed to prison were treated in the same manner as I was. Some of them had died from prolonged exposure in their cells. Some had become deranged, and a few had committed suicide.

With further brooding on my situation, I thought it pretty hopeless, and decided to offer to serve as a non-combatant. This, of course, meant wearing the hated uniform and taking orders in the British Army, in which I had little trust that they would not try to change my non-combatant status of baker into a combatant role. I felt the humiliation of compromise. But I was still determined, whether by direct refusal of orders or by stratagems of evasion - quite an art in armies - not to kill or hurt any humans deemed in the circumstances of the war to be of Britain's enemies.

After the few days of looking after me and the other prisoner patients in the adjoining cell compartments of the hospital my Wildean doctor went off to other duties. He was replaced by another medical officer a lot less friendly and conforming more to the Haw-Haw traditions of the British ruling class, military and civil. Though I was still coughing much and weak in body and limb, he soon had me out of bed, and, as he teased me, half jokingly, shaping something like a soldier. This was given countenance now by my having donned the King's uniform.

I was escorted from the hospital to a new cell allotted me, this time with the comfort of moderate heat. For a few days I was left confined to the cell, with the meals brought me by an orderly. I was now shut in not only by the walls of the cell, but by the more constricting and repellent bonds of the hated uniform. I was now feeling the torments of the self-degraded, and like many another sensitive to degradation I sought solace in philosophising.

Chapter 2

Up to the recent turn of events that had landed me in the prison hospital my experiences in captivity had not imposed any great strain on my will to endure further. The sparse and unappetising diet was a trial, as was also the lack of communication with the outside. I have since read of periodicals, including newspapers and more recently of radio and television being available to convicted prisoners in some jails. For most of my time in prison the only reading matter I was permitted was the Bible. This holy book had earlier become the last resource of my reading. I had found its theology crude, its morality shallow and contradictory, its cosmology absurd and its history folklorish and dubious.

For a few weeks in Wandsworth I had been allowed a book at a time from the prison library. The book was brought to you in your cell by a favoured prisoner permitted this kind of work. I envied him his privilege, but as he was always accompanied by warder I could not engage him in conversation. The selection of books available seemed a celebration of the British Empire and its builders.

And now, discharged from the prison hospital it seemed I was back again in solitary confinement. But there was the difference this time that the cell furniture of plank-bed, bedding, table and stool were not removed during the day from my cell. Another difference was that in serving the meals through the door aperture you were now allowed use of something like normal utensils. In my previous spell the utensils served were a leather plate, a rubber mug and something of stiffened leather as cutlery. The removal of the laces from my boots and the braces from my trousers were further measures, added to the meals precautions, against attempts of suicide.

The most significant difference in my confinement this time was the visit of the medical orderly to my cell twice a day with medicine. He was communicative only to the extent that I was to regard myself as in convalescence. I have already referred to the lack and dreariness of the diet and the absence of news from the outside as being sorely-felt hardships of the confinement, and now hardly conducive to quick convalescence. But perhaps more onerous than these was the persistent vigilance. I thought it clumsy, the furtive shuffling supposed to be secret, outside the cell door, and the long, too eager peep through the spy-hole. Since my arrest in London I had now had several months of surveillance of one kind or another, and probably had become particular or fastidious about it. This crude surveillance, I must have thought, was without style.

I would have recalled the early days of my detention, awaiting court martial at Winchester, how, when I had occasion to go to the toilet or the wash-house

I was accompanied there and back by a guard, a fully accoutred soldier with buttons and badge shining, who made quite a ritual of our progress the purpose of which the undiscriminating would have thought could have been accomplished by a leisurely or informal saunter. Then, on the morning of my court martial there was my escort of two fully armed infantrymen, their rifles shouldered with fixed bayonets. On the way from my cell to the courtroom and at my appearance before the court and on the return to the cell they were at my side, their punctiliousness being matched by the contorted mien of the three officers constituting the court. They were seated bolt upright at a table, their visages set and styled like the stiff gestures of the escort, calculated apparently to impress the sinner or culprit with the awe due the Tablets of Stone.

For me all this ceremonial was heady, but certainly not daunting. Here was I an impoverished emigrant from Ireland that had laboured in a London lead-works now exalted to feeling important, at the very centre of military ceremonial. So much effect had this on me that in my physical movements with my escort I was now responding to the rhythm of their paces, the postures of their strutting. And my responses were not just physical. It was elevation or energising of spirit as well as of muscle. In the course of the proceedings I had been asked by the chairman of the court, as he mustered all the resources of military portentousness, if I did not feel a moral obligation to serve militarily the country that had brought me over from unemployment in Ireland to give me work and a living. I replied with equal hauteur and spirit that I felt no obligation whatever to fight for an imperial power that had so misgoverned my country that it had now no employment to offer many of its people and thus provide them with a living there.

When the brief court martial proceedings ended the chairman, an officer of captain rank, announced that the decision of the court would be promulgated. The ritual of promulgation is one of the higher ceremonies in military practice. On the morning of the event I was escorted by a pair of armed infantrymen on to the centre of a field. The regiment, of about a thousand or so, was drawn up to make a square enclosing the area. On to the field near the centre came a cavalcade, with the mounted commanding officer, his aides and escort. At a bugle-call and command the regiment came to attention, and the commanding officer read out the findings of the court martial. He announced I had been tried by court martial for disobeying a lawful military command, found guilty and sentenced to two years with hard labour.

I learned later that the purpose of this promulgation ceremony in which the regiment is involved is to impress the whole unit, rank-and-file and officers, with the majesty of the military law, and to act as a warning and deterrent to all concerned. For me it meant neither warning nor deterrent. Rather it brought a further elevation of the spirit; perhaps, if my custodians were describing it from my enspirited march-off from the parade-ground with my escort, an inflation of my ego.

And now, in this military section of Wandsworth prison, in what was looking like my second spell of solitary confinement, I am sure I reflected again on my experiences of the military unction, culminating with the promulgation, and the feeling of something like euphoria which they induced in me. Shakespeare, in his play, Henry V., had asked:

> *And what art thou, thou idol ceremony?*
> *Art thou ought else but place, degree and form?*

But that was to miss the point about ceremony. One might as well have asked about a man: what was he but the sum of his parts?

We should know that ceremony is more than the sum of its parts, more than the insignia and robes of office, the bunting and panoply of pageant. It has its élan or spirit that inspires and sustains. And its spell has been potent in all epochs, in all classes, often made the expression or vehicle of mere vanity, often of vulgarity and depravity, and perhaps at times in a strange way, of magnanimity. For instance, in history at times it could have been as much out of a kind of compassion for the condemned as from their judges sense of justice or vindictiveness that men and women that could have been quietly dispatched in lone dungeons were permitted to make this departure in populace-drawing ceremony with the town's highways resounding to the tumbrils and the drumbeats and the exit made high in the town square. Even in the Roman arena, with among the audiences the emperor and court entourage, the pomped spectacle that set ravenous beasts to rive and devour Christian martyrs could perhaps have betokened the imperial favour in ceremony vouchsafed the martyrs that otherwise could have been got rid of quietly and as effectively in the dark vaults of their prisons.

The poet Byron perhaps was pondering such imperial magnanimity when he wrote of Nero seeming to deserve the tribute of flowers strewn on his grave by an unknown –

> *Perhaps the action of a heart not void*
> *Of feeling for some kindness done when power*
> *Had left the wretch an uncorrupted hour.*

And among the martyrs themselves in the Roman arena be sure there were those that welcomed such spectacular martyrdom destined to transmute the roars of brute hunger and the answering lust of the circus mob into Te Deums and Benedictions, later to be vaunted in chancel and choir. There be few who don't hanker after glory. And how is that state or desideratum to be expressed without ceremony? Another English poet, Gray, has written that *The paths of glory lead but to the grave*. But the paths are so often taken for the glory deemed to abide beyond it. This has been, and continues to be attested by our patriots, and, at a less heroic level by pious philanthropists who contrive to carpet the path with wills and codicils of bequests, to be duly recorded on a brazen plate or other public memorial.

My thoughts could be thus given to England's poets, even in an English prison. My father used to say that whilst for an Irishman to quote the English poets might seen like turning the other cheek to Albion, that country had so many quotable poets quotation could range far without touching the compound of imperial jingoism, with its main custodians, Shakespeare at one end, Kipling at the other.

Along with my whistling of opera tunes, another recourse I practised in prison to relieve its tedium was my reciting well-remembered poems, an indulgence learned from my father, himself with some facility in verse-making.

Such were some of the thoughts that came to me in my sojourn in the so-called convalescent cell in Wandsworth, and which had to await more propitious times for something like proper wording. It was much later, indeed, long after I had read and thought to some extent on human achievements in all forms of art and invention, and in the testaments of creeds and codes, and conceived them all in terms of pageantry, ceremony that sought its circus or arena and possibly a posterity to commemorate and maybe perpetuate it.

But in my 'convalescent' cell there were now more urgent matters claiming my attention. It was, I think, on my third day there I was visited by the officer-doctor I was last under in the prison hospital. He gave me a rather cursory examination and communicated more to the accompanying orderly than to myself that I was now recovered and fit for duty. I tried to elicit from them what my duty was to be. I reminded them I had volunteered to work as a baker, and I had been waiting to know when and where I was to start work. The only answer I got was that I'd receive an order in due course.

Shortly after breakfast the next morning I was visited by a non-commissioned officer, a sergeant-major, accompanied by a corporal. The sergeant-major informed me that as I had been pronounced medically fit I would now have to turn out for parade and drill. The corporal would bring me to the Quarter-Master's stores to be fitted with equipment. This turn of events was as much a shock to me as was the confrontation on the evening I was divested of my prison clothes and left naked in the cell with the army uniform.

In vain I argued with them that I had not volunteered or agreed to drill or handle military equipment. The sergeant-major explained forcibly that all servicemen, whether bakers, engineers, tailors, medical servicemen, even doctors and veterinary surgeons, had to be taught drill and the handling of arms, if only to know how to defend themselves. The corporal, much less belligerent than his colleague, tried in a chummy way to make this seem reasonable to me. I showed clear signs of baulking and withdrew from them to the back of the cell. I thought they might have attempted seizing me and forcing me to be fitted for parading and drilling. Apparently not sure themselves how they should deal with a recalcitrant now with a record in disobeying military commands, they withdrew, and I was again left alone in the cell. I had the rest of the day to myself, barring the calls at the cell door with my meals; and I had thus time to ponder on the new situation.

I knew they would not allow matters to stand this way for long. I had no objection to drilling, or, indeed, to the handling of arms. I recalled I had joined the Irish Volunteers in 1914 and had paraded and drilled in the Third Dublin Battalion, and on Sundays had gone on route-marches and manoeuvres in the Dublin Mountains. At the time we had no opportunity of handling arms, but we were eager to do so. I remembered it was probably as much the physical exercise part of the drilling as the patriotic response to serve my country that had attracted me to the Volunteers. Indeed, the drill part of military training would now be a welcome relief from this long tedium of cell confinement.

As to the handling of arms I had no objection to that as such. I was not a pacifist; and from my contacts with professed pacifists in prison I was not much impressed either by them or their doctrine. I could accept that there were those conscientious objectors who had taken a stand on pacifism and had suffered much even to death, who were worthy of acclaim. But I would prefer to believe that they took their stand in assertion of their own integrity rather than in defence of a doctrine (pacifism) which I regard when pushed to the extreme of an absolute as being contrary to the universal instinct of self-defence.

The next morning, after the meal had been served, I was visited again by the sergeant-major, accompanied this time, not by the friendly corporal, but rather the Wildean medical officer. The latter set the tenor of the conversation to follow. He spoke softly to me in his lyrical way, as though metered by the sonnet, and even the brusque non-commissioned officer felt constrained to attempt falling in line, I became the dour one of the trio. The medical man coaxingly tried to convince me that in trying to persuade me to parade and drill the army was in no way failing in their part of my undertaking non-combatant service. The substance of his pleading, previously put less persuasively by his colleague, was that all servicemen, whatever their function, required to be trained if only for purposes of self-defence. The army authorities, he explained, felt this an obligation on their part. After further talk I felt I could read from what he said something like an assurance that in due course I would be posted to working at my trade.

So I agreed to turn out and drill. Later I was escorted to the equipment stores and fitted with webbing equipment, formed of braces round my shoulders, belt round my middle, with attachments at each side of my chest as pouches for bullets. At the tails of the equipment were a scabbard for bayonet, a haversack for rations and other fixtures for utensils. At the back of the equipment, to be carried at the shoulders was the great pack that could carry anything from parts of clothing and toilet needs to blankets - the whole with the emergency rations designed to furnish one's board if need be.

The equipment was not thus fully made up and supplied for use when I put it on in the quarter-master's stores. But there was enough of it in bulk and weight to impress me with its symbolic meaning, that I was now in harness to Britain's war chariot, a vehicle then with much more urgent calls on it than to be bothered to deposit me in the sequestered arbor of a bakehouse.

Though now drilling part of the day with squads of other prisoners there was hardly any lessening of the consciousness of confinement. Most of my time still went in single cell isolation, and when drilling or in other contacts with other prisoners there was the rule strictly applied of no communication. The prisoners exercised much art in outwitting this regulation. Unlike the prisoners I had encountered in the civilian part of Wandsworth, composed as they were of conscientious objectors and civil law-breakers or the commonly-called criminals, these prisoners in military detention were army lawbreakers. They were composed of convicted deserters, absentees without leave, and offenders put away for serious crimes of violence, theft, arson and other serious offences in army service. Some of them had deliberately committed their crimes, preferring to undergo the subsequent detention to being drafted for service in France or other war theatre. Some had already had war service, some of them wounded and suffering from shell-shock, and now ready to venture almost anything rather than be drafted again to the war.

In my contacts with them in the drilling I got to know a little of some of their histories. In their efforts to evade serious military service their attitude generally was that of bravado. They had elevated to a duty what they called dodging the column. My first reaction to them was contempt. I took it, unlike me they were Britishers, and unless motivated by principles against the war in which their country or empire was involved, which was unlikely, I had to regard them as shirkers. I was to discover that when some of them got an inkling of my particular history of military disobedience, they took the same view of myself, that I also was simply shirking war service. I was saddened to think though that they thought none the less of me for that. They could hail me with whispered salutation: 'Good Luck, Paddy', feeling no doubt I was one of themselves.

For sometime this gave me much to worry about in my cell. Had I really fallen or was I likely to fall so far? When I recalled some aspects of my conduct since the start of my detention by the British Military I was not so satisfied with myself. I recalled how I had allowed the authorities to be misled about the matter of my religion. At my early detention in Winchester I had been asked by the officer in the guard room what my religion was. He was entering particulars about me for record purposes. I replied simply that I did not go to any church. I understand he entered me as Church of Ireland, apparently meaning I was a member of the church of which the great majority of the Irish people were members. This, unknown to me, was later changed on my sheet to Roman Catholic, and it was as such I was described when, after the court martial and promulgation, I was lodged in Wormwood Scrubs, my first prison. During my first days there when I learned I was so described I thought I should take the first opportunity of correcting the mis-statement, and re-affirming that I was not a member of any church.

On further reflection I decided to say nothing about it. I was now realising I was in for a spell of solitary confinement. The warders had made this plain by removing from my cell every morning the sparse furniture of plank-bed, table and stool. It had also been indicated by the removal of the laces from my prison boots and braces from my trousers. Those precautions, along with the utensils permitted me the leather plate and rubber mug and the non-metal cutlery, had their own meaning, concern that I would not attempt self-destruction.

In these circumstances I reflected that in leaving my description of Roman Catholic alone I would probably have facilities for going to religious service at least once a week, and that would mean a break of half an hour or so from the loneliness of solitary confinement. I did not at all like the idea of pretending to conform to a belief in which I no longer believed. But it was a temptation I did not succeed in overcoming; and when my first Sunday in prison came I permitted myself to be led along with other prisoners by warders to the prison chapel. The service was much as I had earlier in my life been accustomed to, the low mass with brief sermon, with a number of the prisoners and warders taking holy communion. There was no singing at the service; and the surveillance of the warders in the chapel was as strict as it would have been in any other parts of the prison where prisoners were gathered.

A few days after I had a visit to my cell from the Catholic prison chaplain. He was Irish and if I remember rightly his name was O'Connor. Reluctantly I agreed to his suggestion that I should go to weekly confession and holy-communion. In agreeing to do this violence to convictions I saw it as an opportunity perhaps of getting some news about my parents and home, through the good offices of the priest. I had not heard anything about them since before the court martial. After the court-martial's verdict had been promulgated I had written my parents informing them of the result. Since then no correspondence had passed between us, and they knew nothing now of my whereabouts.

For the several weeks more I was in the Scrubs Prison I went to the weekly confession, the Mass and holy-communion. But I found these temporary and brief releases from my cell had brought little respite from the brooding and depression I was feeling in confinement. The priest was of the ascetic type, greatly absorbed in the formularies of his vocation, and apparently with no interest in politics or worldly affairs generally. He had not succeeded in getting in contact with my parents; and, indeed, I came to regret I had said anything to him about them or their circumstances. I had told him, after he had questioned me, that when I left Dublin my father was only partly employed, and that I had been sending my mother part of my wages when I was working in the lead-works. The priest was aware that if I became a serviceman, even in non-combatant service I would be paid service-pay and my mother would receive a weekly pay allowance. This had been another worry that was troubling me. I could have been of help to my home had I agreed to soldier. As against that, my father, who was a strong nationalist, would not be pleased at my soldiering for Britain; and as for my mother, whilst she might not have had much concern politically, she would certainly worry at my undertaking soldiering risks in the war situation. At times I had put these concerns at the back of my mind in face of worries nearer hand; and now the priest had raised the question if, indeed, my first duty was not to my parents in their need rather than to my stubborn assertion of political principle.

I disregarded the implied suggestion of the priest, and for the remainder of my time in Wormwood Scrubs I was to hear nothing from him of my parents or my home. The religious observances on the Sundays had brought but short respites in the confinement otherwise unbroken on the sabbaths. When I was transferred to Wandsworth I continued going to the Sunday morning service, but not to confession or holy-communion. I was not keen on becoming acquainted with the Catholic chaplain there, and I cannot recall ever having met him. I had come more and more to regret having made a hypocrite of myself by pretending observance of a religion in which I no longer believed.

In the military section of Wandsworth Prison, in which I was now confined, beyond the religious services there were no parades or drills on the Sundays.

At first the routine of drilling that started on the Monday and went on for the rest of the week was a relief from the dreary cell confinement of the sabbath. But the relief wore off as the drills kept repeating their boring patterns. It was mostly foot drill in a comparatively small square, bisected in angles with high walls and higher buildings outside. We made lines and squares in our drilling. The movements were timed with sharp commands, and the configurations made lines, squares and angles.

In some of the drills we handled rifles. We were each furnished with one, but without bullets or bayonet, which, I suppose, was part of prison safety or security precautions. The drill with rifles was even more exacting than that with our limbs and bodies. If the enemy was to be despatched properly it had to be done in strict accordance with Euclidean principles. He had to be shot at the proper angle. Even if neither your enemy nor yourself knew anything about mathematical laws they had to be impressed on him where it sunk in most effectually. In our rifle drill the drill sergeant or corporal had to have the mathematical eye to discern if the angle at which the rifle was held veered unduly to the acute or the obtuse. This, of course, was important when aiming at the enemy, but at least equally important was the rifle's angle when presenting arms, the courtesy salute given passing officers or inspecting notabilities.

In ruminating in my cell on these aspects of the drill I am sure I thought back to my school days and my tortured efforts to learn mathematics. In that context I was most likely to recall Brother Hynes. He heroically had tried to imbue us with his own love of pure or virgin trigonometry. He loved triangles, apparently for their own sake. He was not at all interested in the triangle at work, say in planning the architecture of a building or the working of a machine. For him a triangle at work seemed something of a desecration, a thing of perfection and beauty made vulgar by being put to use. I could have imagined him, though religiously devout, believing that the triangle was the true symbol of the Trinity or God-head, its three divine and equal apexes pointing, perhaps some would think ironically, the truths of the pagan Euclid.

At school I certainly lacked such love or reverence for pure mathematics. I wanted to see the angles and curves at work in some practical construction, say, as was my great yearning at the time, in a bicycle, or a set of mechanical trains.

If my thoughts in that cell on the drill routines had turned to recollections of my school days they would surely have dwelt on the agonies of my homework on the trigonometry lessons. I often worked well into the night; sometimes taking Euclid to bed with me. How I would warn the student with little aptitude for trigonometry against taking triangles to bed with him. They are likely to persist in making their points perhaps well into the early hours, leaving the student hardly eager to face more of the like in class that day.

Brother Hynes's devotion to the triangle had made me think of the Indian fakir and his bed of nails; and when I thought of the Brother trying to enthuse others about his triangles I pictured the fakir going about collecting beds with nails to furnish a lodging for devotees.

Perhaps in that cell I thought also of Brother Hynes in his other teaching role in the Brothers' School in Dundalk. He took our group at Latin. Some of us were being trained as altar-boys, some as members of the junior choir. I was being tutored for both altar and choir. At the time I was regarded as having a fine boy-soprano voice. I liked singing and came to fill a leading role when the choir gave recitals. Most of our public singing was at services of Mass and Benediction in St. Patrick's Cathedral. The new Choir-Master there was the organist Herr Heuermann. He was a German not long resident in Dundalk. He had difficulty in understanding spoken English and his knowledge of Latin seemed equally poor.

It became a prank or joke in our choir deliberately to mispronounce or substitute words in the hymns when singing to his organ playing. Perhaps cause for this might also be found as our reaction of irreverence to the excessive indoctrination of piety then a marked feature of education in the Christian Brothers. I should imagine though our main purpose in sometimes parodying some of the hymns in the services was to make fun of the over-solemn organist and his often laughable attempts to make himself understood to us. Of course the parody version of a few words would be sung sotto voce, so they would not be distinguished beyond the choir's precincts. At this time it happened that our bakery had just been given sole agency for the manufacture of *Hovis* bread in the town. Many of the boys in the choir and the school were the sons of local shopkeepers and traders, and we were used to ribbing one another about our families' products or goods. On this occasion we were singing at evening Benediction in the Cathedral. To the intoning of the Litany we were making the response: *Ora Pro Nobis*. I was leading in front of the choir, but could distinctly hear some of the boys near the organist at the back mutter: *Oh Hurrah for Swift's Hovis*, and repeating it in the responses.

I was not alone in hearing and understanding this profanation of the hymn and the liturgy. It happened that Brother Hynes had ascended the stairs to the organ loft and had listened from a niche to judge how the boys were progressing in their pronunciation of the Latin in the hymns. It had become quite a scandal in school the next day, when our greatly shocked trigonometry and Latin Master brought along the Brother Superior to the rounded-up choirboys for a full dress enquiry. Brother Hynes more than hinted that I had prompted the gross piece of irreverence if not as a sales slogan for our bakery then as sacrilegious disrespect for religion. I was already being suspected in this regard by some of the teachers and pupils in the school, their misgivings or suspicions probably being heightened by the reputation my father had gained in certain quarters in the town for highly unorthodox views about religion. From that time on until I left the school Brother Hynes was to take a missionary interest in my spiritual affairs. I took his bothersome zeal as being as much resentment at my indifference or scorn at his triangles as concern for my immortal soul.

Later, when I had learned a little about the practical work of the triangle and its significance in an area much broader than the Christian Brother's trigonometry class I could have smiled perhaps that I had got my own back. I was learning of the triangle's function in calculating the distances of inaccessible bodies from the earth and how the measurements and discoveries of mathematicians from Copernicus to Galileo had disproved the geocentric theory of the universe as taught by the Church and by Brother Hynes and his colleague Christian Brothers.

In my cell cogitations on the barren mathematics of the drilling in Wandsworth a heavy thread recurring in the pattern was the reminder of my number. Every serviceman had a number. This was his ultimate identity, not so much his name, still less his home address. The number, along with the name and the unit, was stamped on a disc, always to be worn, like a scapular, round the base of the neck. The purpose of this was to effect identification of the body should the serviceman fall in severe disablement or death. The repetition of my number by drill officers or others of the surveillance riled me perhaps more than the drill itself.

The number had seven or eight digits, and though a long-tailed demon to me at the time I have long forgotten the digits and their order. Indeed, I have long forgotten much of the misery, humiliation and shame endured in those prisons.

I was in this Wandsworth Military Prison about five weeks when, with other prisoners, I was transferred by motor truck to the Aldershot establishment operating under the same Army Police Authority. It was known as the Glass-house, and had the reputation of more than ordinary prison severity. It had the name of its regime being so severe often its inmates volunteered to go on drafts to the war areas to escape the rigours of the place. My experiences were to confirm this general impression of the harsh discipline and bullying that went on there.

But there were features about the place that, compared with the Wandsworth Military Prison, made the Glass-house, at least for me, the more endurable of the two. At our arrival there the very look of the place with its great vistas of vast buildings and broad spaces that seemed abutting an open country gave the impression that confinement here could hardly be so constrictive as that experienced in other penal establishments. Here one got glimpses of fields, their green landscaping the prison buildings and neighbouring barracks and other army installations across the Aldershot plain.

In the deprivation felt by the senses that is at the core of prison hardship, which of the faculties, sight or hearing, suffers the more? For me it was sight, when in solitary confinement in Wormwood Scrubs I was able to mitigate the soundlessness of the cell isolation by heavy pacing on the strong flags and bursts of whistling, the latter usually a spirited obligato to the rhythmic percussion of my feet. In the Verdi arias and other martial pieces, suited to my brio mood of defiance at the time, I had an inexhaustible repertoire. My recitals, I am sure, were not all bravura. Some passages must have been gracia mood, if only in gratitude to the prison cobblers that could turn out instruments to stir such articulation from the cell floor.

Against such recourse or resource available to the ear in the solitary confinement of the Scrubs the eye had little prospect there, its range limited by the four walls of the narrow cell. The end wall opposite the cell door had at its top near the ceiling a narrow oblong window with bars across it that made the patch of early winter sky visible a contorted grey, a surliness set not to disclose anything going on in the world without, not even the passing of a bird.

Whilst there was this broader landscape in Aldershot, in the part of the prison where we were incarcerated the conditions were much the same as before. Each prisoner had his narrow cell, the standard of the meals, the routines of cleaning and tidying, the visits to the washhouse and so forth, were much the same as before. But outside, in the parades and drills, and in the allocation of duties called fatigues, we were to see welcome changes from the former routines. The Aldershot Glass-house, being much larger than Wandsworth or any of the other military detention prisons, it had many more prisoners and warders or guards. Carrying on much more varied activities, it seemed something of a punishment clearing house for army defaulters preparatory to their allocation to drafts for active war service.

As regards the drilling the greater space at Aldershot permitted movements and manoeuvres of bigger numbers, and for the finish-off phase of the military training there was nearby the extensive rifle-range where the prisoners were put through their final drills of shooting practice, grenade-throwing and bayonet-thrusting. For breaches of the regulations about drill, for disobedience and other infractions of the prison code there was the punishment of pack-drill. This entailed the prisoner turning out accoutred in full equipment with fully laden pack on back topped by rolled blankets. Armed with a rifle he would be ordered rapid succession of movements. Sometimes the prisoner would be the sole one on parade with the drill officer whose staccato commands would involve the prisoner in quick-changing evolutions deliberately timed to exasperate and exhaust him. The barked commands of the drill officer added humiliation to the exercise.

In the squad in which I was put in Aldershot, comprising prisoners whose cells were located in the same wing of the prison, much of the surreptitious talk whispered at the drills was about avoidance of pack-drill and the chances of being put on fatigues, as working parties were called. The most envied of the work parties were those ordered for duties in the cook-house and the ration stores. The Army's regular commissariat service normally did essential work in such departments and in sanitary and general maintenance duties in the prison. But at this stage of the war, with ever-growing demands for men needed in the battle zones, even the staffs of prisons were being combed for the drafts, and recourse was being made of prisoner labour.

So of the squad in which I drilled half a dozen or so of us were made a group for fatigue work. We would be relieved of drill for a few hours or more and marched off by the corporal or other drill officer to do maintenance or repair work of different kinds. The work, usually of a dispersed kind, was of its nature not susceptible of the same rigorous supervision as was the drilling. We, therefore, had freer opportunities for discrete, if brief, chats among ourselves. In this way I became more acquainted with some of my fellow-prisoners in the fatigue party. One of the jobs given the party that lasted for several days was at digging and constructing earth works at the rifle-range at one of the far ends of the prison. The earth works were being constructed like well-designed trenches with something like living and storing facilities.

Though we had thus freer chances of communicating with one another than when drilling in the squad, there were still certain constraints operating, imposed on us by ourselves, each cautiously measuring out the degree of self-disclosure. I suppose this is inevitable in prison life. After all, its essence is confinement, its main effect enmeshing the soul of the confined. Thus in my squad I was known, not by my name but by the cognomen Paddy, referring, of course, to my nationality. We had a Welshman in the fatigue party, and the sole name he was known by was Taffy. Often in prison the tendency of the prisoner to bestow a nickname on a colleague will have to do with the prisoner's according the colleague the anonymity he is anxious to preserve for himself.

Perhaps there is another aspect to nicknaming in prison. In our work-party we had already an Irishman, myself, a Welshman, two Jews and a few Englishmen, nearly all of them with nicknames, but their family or other histories unknown. Had we had a Scotsman I have no doubt he would have been known as Scottie or Jock, even if it had been bruited he was titled scion of a lordly Scottish family with pretensions to royalty. Such is likely to be the working democracy or levelling rife in that levelled class in all societies, its down-and-outs.

At our trench-digging work in the fatigue party we had chances to dig a little into one another's case histories. I became a bit familiar with a young Jewish prisoner we knew as Gev. This was part of a long Russian-sounding name that I have forgotten. I think the shorter version was kept up to distinguish him from his co-religionist Lev, which was short for Levi or Levinsky, a much more volatile or outgoing member of our work party. Gev was one of the early conscripts who already had war service in France, was wounded there and being given home-leave over-stayed it to hide himself in his community in East London. Like myself he was caught by the redcaps and was now paying the penalty, the most poignant part of which must have been his day-to-day anticipation of early posting to the draft and return to the horrors of the firing-line. Gev was one of the few I met in prison that had political ideals. He was a Zionist, and he regarded the Jewish campaign in Palestine as being of the same character as the republicans' struggle in Ireland. He was not a pacifist, but his heart was not in Britain's war against Germany.

Lev was an altogether different kind of character. He was about the same age as Gev and myself, in the early twenties, but talked as though much older and as with worldly experience to which neither of us had yet attained. He had been committed to Aldershot for offences in connection with the irregular disposal of army property. In the squad guesses were made as to the particulars of Lev's delinquencies, but that they were all concerned with property seemed to be confirmed in observations of him in the prison. It was noted that whenever on the drills he saw a piece of army property, say, a truck or other machine, article or fixture he could not forbear from estimating its value, or putting a price on it. He had no interest or ideology about the war. He longed for the war to be over, to be able to resume his former business of buying and selling. He could see a great future trading in surplus army stock and he was offering Gev a partnership in the undertaking.

Lev was the only prisoner I met during my detention who was able to acquire money, cigarettes and matches in prison. He shared the cigarettes with Gev and the Welshman Taffy. Taffy, who was a miner in civilian life, was superior to any of us at digging and other trench work and was regarded as our foreman, though all took orders from the corporal or other officer in charge. Taffy had been wounded and suffered shell-shock in France. Allowed home on sick leave, he had deserted. Arrested, he had been brought back to the unit's Welsh headquarters, court-martialed and sentenced to term in Aldershot. In our wing of the prison we had been wakened several times around midnight by shrieking from his cell. We took it as being lingering symptoms of his shell-shock. We thought it remarkable, though, when he turned out with us on the fatigue next day he would be as lively as ever at the work in the trenches. Perhaps this came from the anticipation and enjoyment he got from secret smokes he managed to get in during the work. The prison authorities regarded his night shrieking and other show of symptoms as malingering to escape the draft. Malingering was common enough in the armed services and took many forms in simulating various illnesses and disabilities.

The explanation of Taffy's nocturnal manifestations of war-shock symptoms may have had other source besides his experiences at the front under shell bombardment. According to himself, some weeks before being wounded, he had been a member of a firing-party in some wood behind the front when, a court martial sentence, death by shooting, had been carried out on a young service man who had deserted in battle and who, according to Taffy, was dragged to execution crying for his mother.

The extent of the smoking and the comparatively free chats in our work party in the trenches depended on the particular corporal or other officer in charge of us that day. There was one corporal very noticeably lax, so much so it was suspected among the prisoners of our squad that it was through secret liaison with him Lev was able to have communication with outside sources and could thus periodically secure money and smoking materials.

In contrast to this easy-going corporal there was another who was exceptionally severe and officious. The officers generally, both commissioned and non-commissioned, seemed anxious to show efficiency and ardour in carrying out the prison regulations rather than being judged lax and perhaps posted for service in war theatre.

It was on a day when the disciplinarian corporal was on duty with us that an event of serious indiscipline occurred in which I became involved. I had been having furtive chats with the Jewish prisoner Gev. We had been talking about affairs and events in the Middle East and in Africa and indeed in Ireland, under the rule of British imperialism. For some days, become accustomed to the more lax supervision of the liberal corporal, we must have allowed ourselves to presume on the tolerance of his disciplinarian colleague as the latter, at the top of the trench, kept an ear to remarks being made to me by Gev about British policy in the Middle East and Ireland. The corporal descended into the trench, confronted Gev and myself and started reprimanding Gev not only for talking but for uttering remarks highly critical of Britain. Gev, instead of humbly submitting to the reprimand, made spirited reply in defence of what he had said. It developed into personal abuse between them, Gev accusing the corporal of over-zealous discipline in harassing and spying on the prisoners. Angered at this, the irate corporal shrieked at Gev calling him a Jew bastard, at the same time raising his arm to strike him. By impulse I rallied to Gev's defence and pushed the corporal aside. As the two of us confronted one another a few of the fatigue party that had been spectators gathered round and separated us, with the corporal fuming at what he now must have felt was something like general insubordination.

Then the more indulgent corporal appeared, to relieve his colleague of duty in charge of our party. The more easy-going corporal was accompanied by a sergeant of the commissariat service who was in general charge of the trench work at which we were engaged. Feeling as much humiliation at the evident signs of indiscipline now apparent to his colleague non-commissioned officer as rage at our contempt of him, the worsted corporal withdrew with threats of due punishment for our undisciplined conduct. We were then marched off and dismissed to our respective cells.

Chapter 3

The next morning after breakfast, served through the cell door, I was given the order to remain in the cell. This was to begin several days of confinement, without parading for drills or fatigues or other intermissions from confinement. I was to learn that the other prisoners involved with me in the trench fracas were similarly being kept to their cells. Probably, I surmised, we were being held isolated prior to being charged in disciplinary court with gross insubordination.

Several days passed, in which, from odd hints from redcaps on surveillance of the cells, I learned of several rumours circulating. One rumour was that preparations were afoot for getting ready a draft of prisoners for dispatch to some war theatre. I reflected that during the course of our working at the rifle-range we had had spells of drilling in the handling of arms. We did rifle firing at targets, grenade throwing with unloaded Mills bombs, and bayonet thrusting at stuffed sacks. These were regarded as final training given to groups of prisoners listed for early posting to the draft. Unusual activity now going on in the prison day and night was to prove the truth of this rumour.

But meanwhile another rumour was circulating. This was to the effect that the prison preparations were in connection with an impending royal visit to Aldershot, perhaps by the King or the Prince of Wales or other member of the royal family. In speculating on this it seemed to me hardly likely the royal visitor to the area would condescend to visit an institution housing some of the worst malefactors in His Majesty's forces. Most likely, I thought, Aldershot being a vast military area accommodating the training quarters of several regiments, the royal visit would be concerned with more worthy purpose, say, a field investiture for conferring noble orders for meritorious services in preparing troops, on the battle-simulated conditions of the Aldershot Plain, for combat in war theatre.

During my detention I had given thought to this institution of the British monarchy, with its flaunted crown, the symbol of Britain's violation and exploitation of my country. I had come to regard with growing scorn the British monarchial system and the contemptible loyalty that sustains it. Bernard Shaw somewhere defined limited monarchy as a device combining the inertia of a wooden idol with the credibility of a flesh and blood one. Surely the inertia to be noted here is the seeming paralysis in British political development that has tolerated the survival of this medieval anachronism into modern times.

Jingoistic Britons like to boast of the highly democratic character of their State. Yet attainment to the highest office of that state is limited to the members of a single family. Long in-breeding and isolation from the commonalty has made of that family a genus of dullards, its generations making no contribution to the genius or talents of the people over which they have been conferred with the office and privileges of reigning. The family has trailed its mediocrity through the centuries.

Thackeray, in his work on The Georges, dilates on the royal incapacity, in one case instancing the inarticulate George who could not speak the language of his subjects. Yet the Georges were to be honoured by having the name bestowed on an epoch, or period enriched by many contributors to knowledge and culture. Even today we have groups that think to honour the architectural and other arts and skills of the period by calling themselves Georgian societies.

After the Georges came a commonplace woman to inherit and exercise the British royal monopoly. She became Queen with the pretentious name of Victoria, a royal cognomen again to be honoured - the sensible would say made ridiculous - by being extended to an adjective coined to distinguish an epoch richly talented; to note but a few of the endowed, in the biological sciences and related philosophical speculation, Charles Darwin, in Literature, Dickens and Tennyson, in music our own Balfe and Wallace.

If we extend geographically the quest for precious metal lustring the times tawdrily titled Victorian, there will be glowing, in sociological sciences, Karl Marx, in the sciences of invention Edison and Marconi, in medical science, Pasteur and Fleming, and, of the arts, to mention music, Verdi and Wagner.

In my recurrent spells of solitary confinement; an example of which I was now experiencing in the Aldershot Glass-house, I suppose it was natural for me to dwell on the less desirable characteristics of my jailers and their institutions. And yet my thoughts were being prompted by less critical moods, to something like pleasant reminiscence, extending even to fanciful enlargement. In my efforts not to make worse the poignancy of my situation I had tried not to think over much about my parents and the other members of the family and their likely circumstances. Now I was disposed to conjure up recollections of them, fanciful reminiscences of them when all of us were younger and life seemed potent of nothing but the pleasant and heartening.

I suppose this mood was an effort to combat what might be the imminent prospect of being ordered out of the cell to be posted to a draft destined for one of the war theatres.

All of us prisoners knew the formalities of that. We had had piece-meal rehearsals of it, the calls at the cell doors, the muster on the parade ground, the roll-call, the check of arms and equipment. Then followed the orders to mount the lorries, and the short journey to the coast for embarkation at the port. In all this there was little of formal address, nothing of romantic oratory that would rouse martial spirit in the paraded soldiers, all of them more or less dispirited from inurement in the hated Glass-house.

In training preparatory to the draft the prisoners would have been made aware that whilst on home-service disobeying lawful military commands brought at worst a term of imprisonment; if committed in war zone, or theatre, as it was called, could, on conviction, bring death sentence by shooting. We were aware that the previous year a group of conscientious objectors had been put on a draft and dispatched for service in France. On refusing to obey military orders there they were court-martialled and sentenced to be shot. The Commander of the British forces in France at the time, Field-Marshall Haig, confirmed the sentences; and but for the action of some members of the British Parliament visiting the French war zone at the time the executions probably would have been carried out. Hurried appeals were made to the Prime Minister at the time, Mr Asquith. His intervention secured remission of the death sentence for some lesser penalty. It was said that had Asquith's successor, Lloyd George, been Prime Minister at the time, it would have been unlikely the objectors would have escaped the supreme penalty. Lloyd George was to prosecute the war with much more vigour and ruthlessness than his predecessor as Premier seemed capable of mustering.

In this latest confinement to my cell I had been able to shut such concerns from my mind, at least for spells when reminiscence and phantasising on earlier, unstressed times occupied me. Part of my prompting to this was my having earlier acquired some writing paper and a pencil. On one of our fatigues I had been passed them by my fellow prisoner Gev. He had purloined them on a fatigue in the Quartermaster's store. This important department of the prison commissariat vied with the cookhouse as a favourite fatigue place. Each was a challenge to the prisoner's thieving capabilities, the volume of the foods or articles to be thieved being limited only by the possibilities of their concealment in the prisoner's clothing.

In the intervals between the furtive redcap inspections through the spy-hole in the cell door I had been using the writing material, a jotter, large enough to make a bulge in a tunic pocket, and a black lead pencil with sharpener. These, when not being used, I kept on my person. I was afraid to try concealing them in the cell, which was liable to be entered at any time and subjected to search by the redcaps. The writing material had become something like treasure, hugged, if not at my breast, then at more accessible and enfolding part of my corpus. There were exceptions to this routine when, on orders to parade for the bath-house, I had to chance hiding the treasure in folds of the bedclothes now tightly packed on the bed-board at the far end of the cell.

My entries in the jotter were more in the character of notes, something like painter's sketches, later to be worked on in broader perspective. They had to be given some detail though, if in later review they were to be intelligible. In case the jotter should fall into the hands of the redcaps I tried in my notes to keep off prison matters, confining my writing to recollected subjects. Anyway prison matters offered melancholy themes for writing.

There was one prison incident or series of incidents which I though I should make notes about. In the Glass-house, as I suppose in prisons generally, it was rare for prisoners to come in contact with the higher officers of the institution. Indeed the general desire was to try to avoid such contacts. Approaches to or by the higher staff usually meant trouble for the prisoner. Generally it will have eventuated in complaints by the lower or non-commissioned officers regarding breaches of discipline by prisoners. The higher or commissioned officers will be glad to leave such matters of prison surveillance to the inferior ranks, the sergeant-majors, the sergeants and corporals.

In the operation of the system the non-commissioned officers come to have considerable power. Dealing directly with the prisoners from day to day they are in a position to make reports to their superiors regarding not only the individual prisoner's disciplinary record but also the progress made in becoming an efficient soldier. This, of course, was largely determined by the almost ceaseless drilling that went on in the Glass-house. Most of the drilling was done in small groups, squads or platoons, and these were supervised by the non-commissioned officers, sergeants and corporals. It was only when a much larger group of company or battalion size was paraded that the commissioned officers came on the scene.

It was thus the lower ranks of officer came to have much of a say when drafts were being prepared for service in the war zones. Among the prisoners there were mixed feelings regarding readiness or reluctance to being posted for a draft. Some felt the prison conditions so harsh they were goaded to volunteer for the draft; others so dreaded being dispatched to war zone they would do almost anything even to the extent of violence to prison property or personnel and even to themselves in hopes of escaping the draft.

On the other hand, of course, among the prison non-commissioned officers the aim was to get the prisoners out on the draft as quickly as possible. The case I heard about and of which I made notes in my cell writing showed reactions to the draft that were unusual, the prisoner wanting to hasten his posting to the draft and the officer desirous of delaying it. The case is an example of some of the surreptitious liaisons between individual non-commission officers and prisoners that sometimes went on under the surface of the very strict regime in the Glass-house.

The prisoner in the case was a private soldier of a London-based infantry regiment doing a term for absence without leave and theft of army property. His parents were French and were in the catering business in London. He himself had been born in England, and with the coming of the Conscription Act in 1916 he was called-up for military service. He had received most of his education in French and spoke that language better than he did English. In consequence it seemed natural that he picked up the nickname 'Froggy'. In the drill squad to which he was posted in the prison he came under the command of a sergeant who had been on active service in France in the early days of the war. He had been wounded and when recovered had been posted to home duties.

When in France, on redcap base duty, he had met a young French woman and the two became lovers. The communicating part of their lovemaking must have been in sign language, for it appears he spoke little French and she less English. Before being invalided from France with wounds from an air raid, the sergeant undertook to keep in touch with his French sweetheart by some kind of correspondence. Returned to England, before being declared fit again and posted for surveillance duty in the Aldershot Glasshouse, he had corresponded with her in a kind of pidgin French. When she responded he struggled with a dictionary to make something of her letters.

Then, settled at duty in the prison, he met Froggy in the drill squad; and soon one of those jailer-prisoner secret liaisons not uncommon in such institutions developed. It was thus Froggy came to supervising the sergeant's cross-channel correspondence translating the letters from the lady-love in

France, and drafting replies for the sergeant to copy in his own hand. For his services the prisoner was remunerated by the sergeant with odd gifts of biscuits and sweets, with occasional cigarettes and matches, probably from the Garrison Canteen.

Meanwhile the lovelorn sergeant was hurriedly and painfully taking lessons in French from a teacher in Aldershot town, the better to deal with the correspondence. He had made some progress when in reading Froggy's drafts of replies to be sent the lady in France, the sergeant began suspecting that the prisoner was subtly injecting his own identity and attempting to advance his own suit in the drafts. The sergeant's suspicions became stronger when the prisoner began gracing the drafts with terms of endearment which the stolid Englishman thought ridiculous and completely out of character (his character). One such expression went: 'I am your little frog!'

'Didn't the French eat frogs? - and snails?' One could have imagined the sergeant fuming. If further proof of the prisoner's duplicity were needed it was furnished in the last draft submitted by the prisoner. What had become a customary endearment was extended and translated 'I am your little frog, and here, away from you, I pine in a dark and stagnant pond, a prison. How I long for the light and warmth of your sun, to lay on the warmed grass and chant homage at your feet.'

It was now plain to the sergeant that Froggy was planning to supplant him in this tortuous lovemaking by correspondence. It was evidenced also in the prisoner's growing efforts, now become enthusiasm, to master the drills and shine in the fatigues. These signs, along with the prisoner's ready conforming with the most irksome of the prison regulations were clear signals that the prisoner wanted posting on the earliest draft. With the known preparations by the Germans at the time for a spring offensive on the Western front the Aldershot drafts had now only one destination, France.

The sergeant was now determined to keep Froggy in the Glass-house and undrafted as long as possible. To this end he kept making bad reports of the prisoner's progress in training and his conduct in general. But Froggy had become such an exemplary soldier he had come under the notice of the sergeant's superior officers, who saw to it he had early posting to a draft for France.

He was lucky in finding the unit to which he had been posted was stationed near the locality in which dwelt the recipient of his ardent prose. Some months later the sergeant was further chagrined to learn that his former partner in the prison liaison and the damsel of their strange suits had been joined in matrimony.

Such was an example of how paper and pencil, in themselves hardly staunching materials, were now propping my spirit in the glum durance of the Glass-house. But the grim prison was anything but rich in such like themes to prompt recourse to paper and pencil. I was anxious to continue such recourse regarding it as a desirable variation in work to have its place in my labour history, which despite the award of the court martial at Winchester had up to now been void of hard or any kind of productive labour. There, confined in the Glass-house cell my daily labour was limited to moving about the sparse furniture and scrubbing the cell floor. The scrubbing was done on knees bent to the floor, a posture symbolic of the humiliation I felt in serving in the prosecution of Britain's war. Yet, on reflection, had I not served the same cause, and even more effectively, when I laboured in the London lead works, turning out material for the machines and munitions of war; and even, when working at my trade at home in Ireland, had I not turned out bread that went to feed farmers and others in growing and transporting food to sustain Britons in that war? Where did involvement in Britain's war begin and end?

Such melancholy speculation was to be eased or banished by resort to pencil and paper and, of course, the choice of theme calling for their use. At school one of the few subjects I was considered good at was composition. I did best when the subject stirred my imagination. I had won prizes in the subject, and, with the Christian Brothers' dedicated encouragement of the oleo graphic arts my trophies were always in the form of holy pictures. These were hailed by my parents with little enthusiasm, and with my ready agreement they were passed on to my aunt Mary, my mother's sister, who was living in our house at the time. She had quite a gallery of them in her bedroom, and the pious lady made special display of the oleograph, the Souls in Purgatory. This displayed a landscape of lurid flames and smoke, with gasping mortals riven on sulphurous rocks and looking upwards, presumably at the distant seat of mercy.

And now, in the solitude of my cell, these recollections of the past were alternating with spells of brooding, with the prospects still looming of a call at my cell door to accompany escort to the tribunal dealing with breaches of prison discipline, or, alternatively, to be ordered on parade for the draft. To stem the brooding the only resort was recourse again to pencil and paper. Recalling the early years in Dundalk was unearthing much data for pencil work and stimulation of the imagination. Even when I was a pupil in the Grande School, the Sisters of Mercy's Kindergarten in the local convent, I found myself involved with persons and events that could well have stimulated the interest of more mature observers.

I was corrupted at an early age, not by the apples of Eden, which loomed later, but by surrender to the gen of our most primal flaw or sin coterminous with our efforts to persist or exist, Greed. Acquisition, biologically and psychologically, is an essential function of our being; and what we judge its excess we call greed. Come from school, my mother would send me out on the town to search for my father. Sending me off she would give me a three-penny piece as pre-paid wages or commission. My surmise as to his whereabouts was likely to be Conlon's public house and grocery establishment. This was his favourite tavern, where he had a kind of status. Conlon's was situated a few premises up on the opposite side of the street where our bakery and shop were established. This was Clanbrassil Street, the principal business thoroughfare in the town.

Conlon's tavern was known as The Temple; and its regular and more prestigious habitués known as Templars. They were usually accommodated (some of their more spiteful critics would have said, domiciled) in the front or Grande snug of the premises, its deep-curtained window looking on decorously to the main thoroughfare. The Temple had the reputation of discharging something like quasi-governmental functions, such as are normally performed by offices of heraldry or registries of titles. A more or less permanent activity of The Temple was research into nicknames, and not infrequently their creation. A goodly number of the town's citizens had nick-names, which in many cases, probably were loathed and held in contempt by their bearers. There were in the town important personages who went in dread of acquiring nicknames. These usually were careful to avoid being seen in the vicinity of The Temple, lest some peculiarity or characteristic of theirs should come under the notice of Templars, with the likelihood of some undesirable nickname issuing. Some of these worthies were known, in their journeys to and from their offices or other places of business in the town to take circuitous routes, through laneways and other undesirable thoroughfares, rather than risk passing The Temple.

On the other hand, there were those of humbler status in the town who, feeling themselves un-noted and nonentities, hung around The Temple in the hope that some eccentricity or feature of theirs would come under observation and be awarded the conferring of a nickname. There was, for instance, the case of the casually employed handyman Tompson. He got work when circuses and hobby horses and swing-boats came to the town and on occasions when sports were held in the Athletic Grounds. He was an able-bodied and nimble man; and groups of spectators gathered to watch him when he started performing acrobatics in the street outside The Temple. He had persisted in his displays of muscular dexterity till, after some days, he was removed by the police for obstructing the traffic. By that time he had so impressed The Templars that he won the cognomen, The Tumbler Tomson.

As sometimes happened this particular conferment was not a unanimous one among The Templars. For one of them, Dr. Flood, a not frequent visitor to the snug and more of an honorary Templar, the nickname conferred on Tomson was rather shallow, a cheap bit of alliteration. The doctor had a pharmacy nearly opposite The Temple. He was a scholarly man, well versed in grammar, and had complained before about the alliterative tendency in The Temple's awarding or conferring of nicknames. He was fond of saying, in effect; that alliteration could grace a point, but over-used it tended to become the poetry of the illiterate.

Of the alliterative tendency in The Temple's awarding or conferring of nick-names the doctor could cite such example as Curly Crowe and The Luxor Lawless. The former, Crowe, was the town's best-known barber and wig-maker. He had been graced by nature with rich curly hair of auburn shade, which obviously suggested the ready nickname. It had been a lazy choice, made without the research or reflection that judicious nicknaming would seem to require. As for the barber himself he so hated the nickname he had had his hair straightened, a process he had to have done in Dublin and repeated at short intervals, the natural tendency of the hair being to curl as it grew. To match his curly locks he had cultivated a mustache that curled upwards at the ends, which, with his robust physique, made him look a bit like Eugene Sandow, the celebrated strong-man of the period. And now, lacking his former curls and seeming all but hairless, Curly was going round looking like a wraith, and all to thwart and hopefully to have cancelled an un-wanted nickname.

As for the Luxor Lawless' nickname Dr. Flood himself may have been responsible for that particular piece of alliteration. Lawless, a youngish man of find upstanding physique, was an employee of the Gas Company. Dundalk at the time was lighted by gas, and Lawless was the head lamplighter. He looked after the lamps in the centre of the town, in the area of the courthouse and the Market Square and streets immediately adjoining. Shouldering his long staff, with the mien of a soldier bracing his weapon, he went his daily rounds, lighting the lamps at dusk in the evening and extinguishing them in the morning as dawn broadened on the town's horizon. These cycles ran with such regularity that people set their watches and clocks on the lamplighter's beats.

But it was not only The Luxor's lamplighting that earned him his nickname. Lawless was an important member of the Emmet Band, a musical combination in the town that had regaled its people over many decades, and had won renown beyond the town and even the county's borders. Lawless played no instrument, but he led or fronted the band, its drum major. The staff he bore in this office was surmounted by an elegant brass bulbous coping. When not parading with his mace-like staff the drum major spent an amount of his spare time polishing his bauble, until it could have been said of it, like the lamplighter's staff, it was giving light to the town. It was consideration of these two roles of Lawless suggested the nickname of The Luxor or just Luxor, the giver of light, of which the Latin word was lux. The choice of the nickname was easily attributable to the doctor, he being versed in the Latin language. The lamplighter-drum-major had no Latin, and when he heard of his nickname's meaning he gloried in it; and if the town's lamps could have glowed with the new fire he put into carrying his staffs, it would have been nigh ablaze.

Dr. Flood's calls at Conlon's snug had more to do with renewing contacts with my father. He was our family doctor; but his visits to our home had not been limited to the occasions requiring his professional services. He was a man of wide cultural interests, some of which he shared with my father, particularly in topics to do with poetry and music. The two would have rapt discussions on these subjects, even on occasions when the doctor's visits had urgent medical import, such as at my mother's accouchements, my own seasonal ailments and periodical illnesses of my grandmother.

Dr. Flood was a prominent member of the Dundalk Orchestral Society, in which he played a string instrument, a violin, if I recollect correctly. In this connection another instance of Temple nickname conferring comes to mind. Again the recipient was a member of the Emmet Band. And this time the conferring or investiture was abortive. The nickname, much to the chagrin of the recipient, didn't take on. The bandsman concerned was the principal drummer. He played the big drum, and, though with little formal musical education, he was regarded as having mastered the instrument. His name was Pious Finnegan, and he had come to hate the Christian name, for he had little piety in him and tended to despise the pious generally.

Still in the vigour of youth, he was working in the coal-portering trade, in which his muscular frame, extending to above the middle height, served him well on the band's parades. His protuberant abdomen and chest gave the big drum unusual elevation; and on gala occasions, when the drummer would have quaffed perhaps a half-dozen pints of porter, the drum was thus furnished a nice springy base for the drum-beats to issue in a furtive rallentando or soft tremolo.

The Emmet Band performed in many repertoires; but its magnum opus was its dead march. It could be Handel's, Beethoven's or Chopin's. Whatever the choice for the particular obsequies, it was certain the march would be played with due dignity and poignancy. Usually when the Band was on parade it presented a gay and colourful spectacle, the members dressed in the uniform of Robert Emmet and the United Irishmen. The bright mien was emphasised by the white ostrich plumes that curled and danced on the black hats shaped like boats turned upside-down, their prows and bows tapering to angles fore and aft. Their coats were of green, with rich epaulets and swallow-tailed. The trousers were white, and their legs narrowed into knee-high black boots.

At funerals this colourful dress, that one could have thought designed for display at festive or celebratory occasion, seemed to make more impressive the solemn corteges the town's people had come to witness, indeed to look forward to. Even the least musical among them watching on the route of the cortege would have divined that it was the musician playing the big drum that created not only the tempo or rhythm but the nuances of expression that breathed the soul of the music and communicated it to the hearers. It seemed extraordinary that a big and robust man like Pious Finnegan could moderate his beats on the drum with such sensitiveness and subtlety.

The corteges usually passed through Clanbrassil Street, with the shops and other places of business closed, and the occupants taken to upper floors to watch the cortege and if the cortege on its way to the cemetery was passing through more select residential area, where some of the quality lived, there would be the same resort to the windows above, the same stir of curtains, maybe to dry unbidden tears.

In the early years of its history it was only for the obsequies of prominent persons in the town that the Emmet Band would be engaged to head the cortege. Such honours were reserved for the higher clergy and prominent members of the Urban Council and the Board of Guardians, and perhaps of the Harbour Board. But with the growing skill and professionalism of the Band more and more of the citizens came to be similarly honoured at their demise. At one time it was feared something like the death wish was on the town. People just wanted to be buried to the strains of the Emmet Band. The situation, it was said, so alarmed the public health authorities they made representations to the Band Committee. It was suggested that the committee should review the Band's repertoires, and if the dead marches could not be abandoned altogether, then, in choosing music for obsequies, choices should be made with greater discrimination. The choices should relate to some rational estimate about the deceased worthies and how the citizens really felt about their departure. In some cases it could well be the music to be chosen would be pieces of celebration or thanksgiving.

The number of dead marches in the Band's library was an index to the townspeople's growing interest in serious music. The trend had been furthered by the assistance or fostering that the Band had been able to avail of at different times when foreign musicians of high professional standards came to reside in the town, some temporarily, in a few cases some to make their home there. They were organists commissioned from time to time by one or other of the local Roman Catholic churches, the cathedral or the churches of the three Orders in the town, the Carmelites, the Redemptorists and the Marists.

It was usual for these foreign musicians come to the town to involve themselves in its musical activities. They became honorary or patron members of either the Orchestral Society or the Emmet Band, sometimes of both. In the case of the Band, whilst not taking part in its public performances or parades, the foreign, and gladly adopted, patrons, would usually serve as advisors and instructors, taking an active part in the Band's rehearsals. They were of different nationalities, German, in one case French, but most of them Belgian. It appears there were great traditions of organ playing in Belgium.

It was this circumstance of foreign and diverse tutoring that came to influence so much the musical range of the Band, particularly in the dead marches. Under the aegis or baton of the French Organist, Monsieur Morrel, Chopin's funeral march was the favoured one to be performed at funerals. Chopin, though a Pole, was also of French stock. When later a German organist came to tutor the Band it was Handel 's march was favoured. Herr Vagt poured scorn on Chopin's music as lacking the solemnity of the great German. Chopin's music was more for the waltz or the mazurka, and indeed for the boudoir.

Even more partisan and emphatic in his choice of funeral march was the Belgian Organist, Doctor van Wanden who had a few years tenure at the organ in the cathedral. In this genre, during his spell with the Emmets he would hear of nothing but the Beethoven. Van Wanden was a Fleming, and he was at pains to emphasise to the Band that Beethoven was of Flemish, not German origin. The name Beethoven was a Flemish word (for beet-garden). The composer's other name was Ludwig, Ludwig van Beethoven, not von Beethoven, which was the German form.

When van Wanden was made an honorary member of the Dundalk Orchestral Society he had such a high estimate of Finnegan as a drummer that he got him to perform in the orchestra's rehearsals. The doctor persuaded the orchestra's committee to extend the repertoire to include some of Beethoven's bigger works, pieces such as the Fifth Symphony. There were important drum passages in that work, particularly in the main theme of the first movement. There was the phrase of the few bars, the Pauken an die Pförte (Fate knocking at the door).

At the orchestral practices the Emmets' drummer came under the spell of the few bars of drumbeat. He brought them into his practices in the Emmets' band-room, repeating them on his instrument and enlightening his colleagues that they were the main theme in the great musical work of Ludwig van. From then on the bandsmen were to hear their colleague talking about Ludwig Van, and at times see him secluded in a corner of the band-room repeating on his instrument this brief but dominant theme in Beethoven's great work.

In The Temple perhaps it was not so much tittle-tattle about the drummer's new preoccupation in the band-room that aroused new interest in him than the news of a bizarre incident in which he was involved. It happened in the parliamentary elections in which the Redmondite Party candidate was contesting the North Louth constituency seat then held by Tim Healy, the All-for-Ireland Party candidate. There was much rancour in the campaigns. Healy was still being vilified as the betrayer of Parnell, and he was equally scathing on his opponents.

On a Sunday at the height of the campaign the Emmet Band was fulfilling an engagement at a sports in the small town of Ardee, around a dozen miles from Dundalk. When the sports came to an end crowds were assembling at both ends of the main street that ran through the centre of the town. The crowds were gathering to hear the rival candidates in the election. Each meeting was isolated from the other by the length of the street. The meetings had commenced and the oratory from both was audible as the bandsmen moved from the Sports Ground to the small square at the centre of the street. They listened a while to the sometimes inaudible harangues coming from the rival meetings.

It happened that the bandsmen were about equally divided in their political allegiances. This was made manifest when they started drifting in two groups from the square, one group going off to join the meeting at one end of the street, the other group moving to the meeting at the opposite end.

Soon the speeches at both meetings were followed by intervals of music as the respective sections of the Band regaled its hearers with selections of patriotic airs. At neither meeting was the music up to the usual Emmets' standards, with the bandsmen divided into the two groups the division made ill-assorted combinations, the brass and reeds and percussion being ill-adjusted in each.

Thus became involved in party politicking in Ardee the bandsmen of the Emmet Band - all but one of them. That was the band's drummer, Finnegan. He had sequestered himself in a corner of the town square, his instrument braced, ready for the well-rehearsed beats, a musician dedicated to his art, and not to be lured from it by the irrelevance of politics.

The musician's discourse in repetitions of the few bars of the Beethoven or van Ludwig theme was hardly one to draw passers-by to the scene. But a bevy of the town's dogs, apparently with finer discrimination, showed interest, and as the drumbeats alternated from the moderato to the forte the dogs' interest became audible in crescendos of yelps and growls. Hearers technically disposed might have termed the performance a big-drum concerto, the accompaniment being furnished by avid members of the canine species. Wags in The Temple might have called it the Bow-Wow Concerto.

Indeed, some of The Templars had come to hear of it and of the drummer's continued preoccupation with playing the Beethoven theme. It was the bizarre ending of the Drummer's musical interlude in the Ardee Square that determined The Templars' decision to command Finnegan to investiture. In the Ardee performance the drummer had varied the playing of his instrument, at intervals making the beats with the one hand, the other extended with its drum-stick in the direction of the still barking dogs. Perhaps the intention of this was the friendly one of seeming to act as conductor in attempting to co-ordinate the dogs' yelps with the drumbeats. But this had the effect of making the din worse. At length, feeling alarm, the drummer's grip on the projected drumstick slackened and the drumstick fell to the ground. It had only gained the ground when one of pack, apparently judging the drumstick as a ball to play with, leaped forward, seized the drumstick and ran off with it.

The whole episode was to become an epic in the annals of both the Emmet Band and The Temple. In the latter it had warranted a ready investiture, and what nickname could they confer on Pious Finnegan but Ludwig van? It seemed an auspicious choice when on the conferring night, under my father's chairmanship, the honours were done the Emmet's senior drummer. For his unhappy, humiliating recital with the unruly curs in Ardee he could now feel richly compensated, even with the loss of a drumstick. Soon he would no longer be greeted by his workmates, and his colleagues and friends in the Band and The Temple with the hated cognomen Pious.

The hope, it soon turned out, was vain. The nickname was too esoteric or remote to gain popular currency, an essential for the survival of any nickname however appropriate and well intended. After a few weeks or so of being hailed by the habitués of Conlon 's Grande Snug as van Ludwig the salutation, reverted to the old greeting, Pious. Soon his appearances in the place dwindled, the lapses lengthening till he was rarely seen there. For one thing he was of different professional class from most of the regular patrons of Conlon's. Generally, particularly among The Templars, the habitués were of the artisan or craftsman class. The head Templar, himself, my father, before becoming a master baker and owner, or part owner of a bakery, worked as a craftsman at his trade. It was during that time, when he was President of the Dundalk Bakers' Society, that he first met some of his Templar colleagues who were then also craftsmen working at their respective trades. The association had come about by their common membership of the Dundalk Trades Council. It was only in later years that non-craftsmen, workers at coal-portering, lamplighting, and in many other industries in the town became organised in trade societies or unions.

Apart from Dr. Flood there were a few others of what were called the professional classes among The Templars. These usually were addressed more formally with a mister, a prefix rarely accorded an artisan. For instance, there was the case of the surveyor Johnstone, an occasional visitor to the snug, and more a friend of my father's than an established Templar. Attracted thither as well by Conlon's malt, reputed the best in town, on his visits to the snug he would usually have earlier imbibed quantities of his favourite liquor. Almost invariably he would be accompanied by his theodolite, in proof that he was still gainfully employed at his profession.

In the town it was not uncommon to see the surveyor make unsteady exit from a tavern to the street and, unsure of his shaky limbs, prop the theodolite on the cobbled path to make a leaning or support post of it, till, steadied on his limbs, he made further progress along the street or across the road. This might be on his way to The Temple, and having arrived there, he would insist on being seated beside my father. They had much in common, notably in their interest in the sciences, particularly in astronomy. The surveyor was fond of discussing the importance of trigonometry in the sciences, the role of the triangle in calculating the distances from earth of the heavenly bodies. At the time Haley's Comet was making one of its infrequent visits to regions above the town's horizons.

When the surveyor, a low-sized, rotund, short-legged man, succeeded in wedging himself and the theodolite beside my father on the usually much occupied bench along the curtained window to the street, he would move up, stretching to my father's ear. The surveyor was more discrete than my father in talking about controversial matters, probably from fear it might be reported to some of the members of the body that employed him, the Dundalk Urban Council. As it happened one of The Templars, John McClure, jeweller, watchmaker and locksmith, was a Town Councillor and Poor Law Guardian.

At one of their sessions in the snug, when the liquor had been flowing liberally among the company, and the surveyor had become less secretive or cautious in his communications with my father their conflab turned on how the great discoveries of Copernicus and Galileo had disproved the Biblical account of Creation. Relaxing a bit from close contact with my father, the surveyor was heard to say: 'Well, Pat, I may still go to Mass on Sundays and an odd time to Confession, but, at bottom, I'm a Copernican.'

Following that there were from time to time discussions among some of The Templars, the less informed in matters of science, as to what was a Copernican. The upshot of it was that Mr Johnstone the surveyor was conferred with the nickname Copper-bottom. The cognomen had, of course, nothing to do with the great Polish scientist whose discoveries in astronomy had so affected earlier teachings in the subject. It likely had more to do with the heavy form and gait of the surveyor, as he so often appeared in the streets, with his theolodite borne clumsily on over-burdened shoulder, and seeming to make more ponderous the heavy body on the short legs.

From his furtive talks with my father in The Temple snug the surveyor may have been thought over-cautious or lacking courage in disclosing his views or opinions. But later he was to reveal a certain integrity in discharging the duties ordered him by the Town Council. The Council had plans to acquire parts of Lord Roden's demesne for artisan housing and local amenities. The surveyor, though sympathetic to almost any proposals to re-house the people living in squalid hovels in laneways and alleys in the town, demurred on the Council's choice of the particular area for the development.

Part of it abutted on to the rear of the dwelling in Park Street, where Johnstone lodged, where from his bedroom was to be viewed a long vista through the demesne, making a landscape of trees and lake water, with birds ever coming and going, the prospect extending far to beyond the Castletown river to the evanescent contours of Slieve Gullion. It was a vista the sight of which, dwelt on in the mornings, often after fitful, tavern-induced sleep, refreshed and inspirited the surveyor, braced him to shoulder his theodolite and essay forth for another day's travail.

He could not think to vandalise the pastoral scene, clearly intended by nature as an offering of balm to soothe man's restless and pecunious spirit. He was an early ecologist; in a world of mad urbanisation, a man before his time.

There were Temple patrons that could be graded between artisans and professional people, such as doctors, solicitors and surveyors. Pat Byrne was one of the middle grade, a journalist working as a reporter for the *Dundalk Democrat and Peoples Journal*. This periodical was the more influential, and considered the better edited of the two local weeklies, the other being the *Dundalk Examiner*. Byrne, a young and ambitious man was an aspirant to Templar status. But he was too brash about it. Vain and flashy, he thought he could write as well as talk his way into a more or less permanent seat in the Grande Snug. Instead, he seemed fated to languish anon in the less select, if larger, snug called the Gobi, at the rere of the premises. The name had provoked uncomplimentary jokes. The more discriminating habitués of the tavern would say the snug was a place to be given the go-by!

The Gobi came into being from the growing clientele who sought entry to the Grande snug. This was a constant problem with which the proprietor, Mr Conlon had to deal. The resourceful proprietor, I believe in consultation with the senior Templars, had decided to section off some of the bar area at the back to make a roomier apartment whither aspirants not thought worthy of entry to the Grande snug could be ushered. Among these would be aspiring versifiers, writers of letters to the local newspapers, and others seeking publicity in print. Then there were the few scribes who, rather than have recourse to the Poorhouse earned a precarious living writing epistles to the Town Council, or the Poor Law Guardian or other institutions on behalf of illiterate townsfolk. In brief, it could be said the Gobi snug was designed to accommodate patrons who could be described as of the lower literati and the lower intelligentsia.

The *Democrat* reporter had been judged as of this class by the senior Templars, and he knew he was not welcome in their preserve, the Grande snug. The kind of reporting Byrne had been kept at for years by his editor was the lowest assigned an apprentice journalist, taking notes at the weekly Petty Sessions in the Court-house and the weekly meetings of the Poor Law Guardians, and, in between, to keep in touch with what was going on in the poultry and fish markets. It was probably in reaction to these lowly commissions, which he considered inconsequential, that he was driven to seek refuge and encouragement among the Templars. He had already been judged by them, and, indeed unalterably, when, over period of some months during which the *Democrat* staff had been depleted by an epidemic in the town, the editor had assigned him the writing the obituaries. Just as he had written florid and portentous accounts of the routine and often trivial happenings in the Court of Petty Sessions and the meetings of the Board of Guardians, he wrote such extravagant obituaries that the mourning relatives reading them would feel astonishment at the wholly unsuspected virtues and talents attributed the deceased and would buy extra copies of the *Democrat* to dispatch to their friends. Pat Byrne wrote much of the illiterates' poetry that Dr. Flood and the other higher Templars called excess of alliteration.

Largely at my father's suggestion the Gobi snug was given a floor covering of sand. This distinguished it from the floor covering of the superior snug, the Grande, which consisted of a thick layer of sawdust. In both cases the provision was not so much to furnish something like a soft cushion for the feet, but rather to take and absorb spits, which in a heavy night's drinking and smoking could, as Mr Conlon often remarked, be torrential. Later when the Women's National Health Association became active against tuberculosis and other infectious diseases, these expedients of sawdust and sand tended to disappear from the floors of taverns.

The choice of sand in the Gobi snug was, of course, intended to justify or give credence to the name given the snug. But, more to the point, it was meant as an ironic shaft at some of the snug's habitués who in their cups essayed in the literary art, some in the hope their efforts might be rewarded with publication in the *Democrat*.

There was the story that at the formal opening of the snug my father, accompanied by some of his fellow Templars and the proprietor, Mr Conlon, stressed the appropriateness of the snug's title. He spoke of Gray's poem, the *Elegy written in a Country Churchyard*. He dilated on the poet contemplating the humble graves of the rural dead, and speculating that if given opportunity and means, some of them might have enriched the store of human achievement. My father quoted the stanza of the *Elegy*.

> *Full many a gem of purest ray serene*
> *The dark unfathomed caves of ocean bear;*
> *Full many a flower is born to blush unseen,*
> *And waste its sweetness on the desert air.*

Chapter 4

The respective floor coverings in the snugs had been the subject of debate in The Temple. The materials, both the sawdust and the sand were being supplied from Doherty's builder's yard and sawmill at the rear of the tavern. The biggest in the building trade, Doherty's had been specialising in sawdust production. Generally in builders' yards sawdust had been considered the waste or offal of timber, shed in the process of timber-cutting. Whatever the species of timber in the sawmills usually its offal went to a common heap, to be shovelled into sacks for the sawdust trade.

In Doherty's that trade was considerable. The town used much sawdust, sacks regularly going to various places of business, to taverns, of course, to butcher shops, where the floor had to cope with the drainings of recently slaughtered cattle and sheep; in brief, to the various places of commerce where traders thought floors, even earthen ones, had to be protected, some from customers' footwear, come perhaps from muddy pasture or from the cattle market, its paddock liberally splattered by the stock brought to sale.

Perhaps it was the growing competition in the sawdust trade induced Doherty's to specialize in it. In Doherty's sawmill's no longer was the offal from mahogany, oak, walnut or the other quality timbers consigned to a common heap with the waste of deal or other low-grade timbers. The customer could now get sawdust that accorded with the best of his furniture and fittings, with his mahogany or oak hall-door, or with the same materials moulded into elegant shop fronts, or bar counters and snug furniture. To extend the range of timbers and their sawdust, the Doherty yard had now a machine that could make sawdust of bushes. It could take unwanted hedges, and gardens' aged briars and gooseberry bushes. More recently the firm had acquired tropical material. Ships were now docking in Dundalk harbour with part of its cargo, picked up in Africa, quantities of cactus-like bushes. These were being discharged at the Dundalk docks to the order of the Doherty firm; a distinctive feature of this species was that its pulp had constituents that emitted an odour of musk. When the pulp was reduced to sawdust and came into contact with the atmosphere, more particularly with anything liquid, the odour became stronger and more pleasant.

The Doherty firm was quick to realize how, with this exotic species and their exclusive machine, they could market saw-dust to outrival their competitors. The firm had many high-class customers, including The Temple, who would be anxious to acquire the special brand of sawdust.

As regards the other important stock in Doherty's Yard, sand, again, the firm could furnish varieties of the material. The quality or constituents of sand depended much on the marine life as well as the geology in the particular part of the coast. Sand, say, from the Annagasson or Carlingford region was likely to be more light-grey or even white than brown. This would be largely determined by the mollusc life in the region. Annagasson had a reputation for its codes, whilst Carlingford was noted for its oysters.

Whilst it was to be sand that would serve as floor-covering for the new snug in The Temple it might seem strange that the title given the place was the Gobi. It was to be explained by the fact that it was the proprietor's own choice. Once my father's proposal that the name of the snug should have some desert significance was agreed, Mr Conlon suggested the Gobi. His reason for that, apparently, was that sometime before a foreign boat called Gobi had docked in the port, and a few members of the crew had visited The Temple. They were natives of some area near the Gobi desert, and they had called at the tavern to deliver message to Mr Conlon from his son, then a missionary priest in the Gobi region.

In the tavern's snugs Doherty's sawdust went mostly to saving floors from patrons' spittle. Now that the firm had varieties of the product it was ready to supply it to accord almost with the quality of the spittle, or rather of the spittle's owner, if, indeed, the term owner be a happy one, since the spitter, however acquisitive an individual, will usually want to disown or get rid of his spit.

At any rate, the Grande snug in The Temple was now being supplied with Doherty's deluxe or best quality aromatic sawdust. Judged with what was now happening in the lower snug, the Gobi, it could be said developments in the superior snug were now taking a strange, one could say contrary turn. In the Grande snug it had not been often that spittle was directed to the floor. Whether it was for sanitary reasons, prompted perhaps by the new Women's Health Association campaign, or out of respect for the sawdust, the cosy-seeming pulp that caressed their feet, Templars could rarely be seen ejecting spittle to the snug floor. Even in prolonged coughing, provoked, say, by strong smoke from a pipe or cigar, the Templar was likely to have recourse to the handkerchief, which, I seem to recall of the times, was then a capacious piece of haberdashery.

But, with the introduction of the musk-bearing sawdust to the snug, that reticence with spittle changed. When it was evidenced that contact of spits with the sawdust incited a stronger and more pleasant-smelling emission of odour the snug habitués became less inclined to husband their spittle in their handkerchiefs and more disposed to ejecting it towards the floor. Soon there was what amounted to an abandonment of handkerchiefs as the habitués abandoned themselves to devouring the subtle emanations being distilled at their feet. In vain did Dr. Flood warn them against the spate of promiscuous spitting. The smokers even had recourse to stronger tobacco, so much were they becoming addicted to the cactus emanation.

At the same time a contrary course was developing in the back snug, where, among the lower orders there, the vulgarity of inhibited coughing was something to be expected. But it was quite the opposite. The sand being furnished the floor there was, it seems, of a kind quite rich in the relics of marine life and almost white in colour. It had probably been taken from the seafront at Annagasson or Carlingford. It turned out that if, during a drinking session in the snug, the sand was spat on in any volume the spittle tended to ferment, to emit a strong smell of fish. This, in turn, tended to become unpleasant even to less sensitive nostrils; and soon there was not only a general desire but resolve not to spit in the place.

There followed in The Temple much debate on these happenings that ensued from the choices of covering for the tavern floors. In the debate's suggestions, some of them were frivolous and such as to be resented by the proprietor as offensive. One wag suggested that the tavern be renamed The Cactus and Cockle. Another patron amended with proposal that The Temple be renamed The Cockle and Cactus. The amender turned out to be a relation of the Cockle-man, who, with his basket of cockles and oysters, plied his trade in the town's pubs.

The Women's National Health Association was an influential body in the town. With patronage of the highest order at the top, it was assured the support of local ladies prominent in social circles. The most exalted social luminary at the time was unquestionably Lady Aberdeen, consort of the Viceroy and Lord-lieutenant, the Earl of Aberdeen. She was a patron and active helper of the Association. The local supporters of the Association included Lord Roden. He was the scion of a family of aristocrats, long established in the town as its principal landowners. The present Lord Roden was the landlord of much land in the town and its near surroundings. Roden held high place in the local Protestant ascendancy, and was reputed to hold exalted positions in the Masonic and Orange Orders.

Though very much a minority in the town's population, the Protestant community, particularly the Church of Ireland section of it, had attained much influence in the upper levels of life in the town, in commerce, manufacturing and the professions.

Lord Roden's demesne flanked the artery of the town's main business streets, running through the town from South, at the railway station to North, abutting on the big bridge that crossed the Castletown River. This artery, made up of a succession of streets, the middle section constituting the town's main thoroughfare, Clanbrassil Street, was about a mile in length. Almost for the whole of its length the artery on its West side was flanked by Lord Roden's demesne. The demesne had two main entrances, the South entrance in Park Street and the North in Church Street. The latter street was so called because its most prominent building was the Protestant (Church of Ireland) Church. It stood right opposite the demesne's North gate and lodge. It was an old granite structure, topped by a slender greenish spire and flanked by a graveyard of old and mouldering tombstones. Among them was one that could have been considered comparatively modern. That was the one erected over the grave of Robert Burns' sister.

This monument, erected by the poet's admirers in the town, stood prominently in the forefront of the cemetery, and through the railings on the low wall between the cemetery and the Church Street, was easily visible to passers by. For a few years my father and some of his Templar colleagues had, on the poet's birthday, the 25th of January, made pilgrimage to the hardly substantial mecca in Church Street. Gathered at the railings near the grave, my father would start a recital of Burns' poems. Coming towards the end of the recital the reciter would turn in the direction of the Roden demesne gate, declaiming from *A Man's a Man for a' That*, rendered, not in the Burns Doric but in the plainer English -

> *Ye see yon birkie, called a lord,*
> *Who struts and stares, an' a' that;*
> *Tho' hundreds worship at his word,*
> *He's but a coof for a' that:*
> *For a' that, and a' that,*
> *His ribband, star, an' a' that,*
> *The man of independent mind,*
> *He looks an' laughs at a' that.*
>
> *A prince can make a belted knight,*
> *A marquis, duke, an' a' that;*
> *But an honest man's above his might,*
> *Good faith he needed for that,*
> *For a' that, an' a' that,*
> *Their dignities, an' a' that,*
> *The pith o' sense, an' pride o' worth,*
> *Are higher rank than a' that.*
>
> *Then let us pray that come it may,*
> *(As come it will for a' that);*
> *That sense and worth o'er all the earth,*
> *Shall make the rank an' a' that,*
> *For a' that, an' a' that,*
> *It's coming yet, for a' that,*
> *That man to man, the world o'er,*
> *Shall brothers be for a'that.*

Some of the ladies prominent in the local branch of the Women's National Health Association had also interest in the more recently established, but less popular organisation, the Women's Suffrage League. One of the best known, and one would have thought the most unlikely of these, was Mrs Chambers, the wife of the Northern Bank's Branch Manager. The presumed unlikeliness of Mrs Chambers' active association with the Women's Suffrage agitation would have had more to do with her husband's sensitive business position in the town. Himself a modest and retiring man, who by his business talents and equable manner had succeeded in gaining a strong position for his bank in the town, was known to be averse to the often rash and even provocative attitudes of his wife in the causes she espoused locally. She was fond of raising controversy, sometimes on topics with little or no relevance to the matters at hand.

Mrs Chambers was a matron with a small family. Still attractive-looking and sprightly, she was able to avail of sufficient domestic help to leave her free for the interests she followed in the town. Her speech when unguarded had some of the quality of the Sandy Row argot, and its content was often of the kind to be heard in the street and pub debates common to that highly partisan area of the Northern Capital. One knowing the area and its mores, and coming to hear her in her less uninhibited moods, would be likely to judge that in marrying the bank manager she had risen to status far above the range usually attained by the denizens of Sandy Row.

There were stories in the town about her sometimes flamboyant indiscretions. As a gesture of her support of the principle of sex equality, she was known to smoke cigars and pay readily the consequence of unseemly upset and general embarrassment at meeting or social occasion. At the time smoking by women was rarely ventured in the town, unless among the few brazen hussies who found entrance to low taverns, when they consorted with soldiers from the local cavalry barracks, or swaddies, as they were contemptuously called. To these exceptions might be added the shawled harridans, who went home from selling apples or other such produce in the streets to make more fumed their hovels with smoking clay pipes and quenching their parched and yellow-toothed mouths with cans of porter.

Both Mrs Chambers and her husband were natives of Belfast. Since their arrival at the Dundalk branch of the bank they were known to be members of one of the smaller Protestant congregations in the town. He seemed one content to leave his creed in the pew on Sunday evening and return for another brief session with it the following Sunday. In the interval one had to get down to the serious business of the week. His wife was not so disposed. In the intervals between the weekly gospel services she thought religion had a place, and the way to make room for it and give it that place was not so much vaunting the merits of one's own creed as pointing the demerits or errors of those espoused by others, more particularly Roman Catholics.

Mrs Chambers attempted this, not by any attempt at doctrinal argument, of which she would have been incapable, but rather by roundabout ways of disparaging innuendo. One subject she liked exercising her prejudices on was the town's arms. The main feature of the municipal arms was the three black, crow-like birds. They were displayed as occupying the whole of the shield, its expanse with not a curl or come-on twirl to intimate that the town was offering the pilgrim-like creatures sanctuary or hospitality. With the three birds displayed on the escutcheon in profile and erect on braced legs, they gave the impression of being on their way out of the town. This impression of their preparing to walk off was unfortunate, since walking was an exercise the crow species performed with little grace, with awkward gait and jerk of wing, made as though to ease the strain of bunioned feet, or in imitation of a buffoon feigning drunkenness.

It was true the town's escutcheon was a poor, some would say shabby piece of municipal arms presentation. Critics that wished the town well wondered at its paucity as a piece of heraldry. Surely that art or science would have had more in the way of nobler fauna, not to mention embellishment to offer the town's founding fathers and their heirs than the three strolling crows, sequestered as they were on the shield with not even a twig to give them a sense of something to grasp or hold on to, much less an angle of branches that would anchor a nest or home for them.

We know from the records of offices of heraldry that their resources in the way of fauna must be inexhaustible. If they haven't models from the real world, then they manufacture them. We are familiar with the griffins, the dragon and the two-headed eagles which heraldry furnishes patentees and their aspirants not to be fobbed off with a mere lion or elephant, much less a sheep or other of the lower fauna commonly displayed on armorial shields, from the pretentious cockerel to the more modest, but industrious, bee.

The town of Dundalk is, of course, in the heart of the Cuchulainn country; and there were many in the town that regarded that character of legend as having been of real flesh and blood, in fact an authentic Dundalk man. They queried: why a trio of common crows on our escutcheon? If we had to have a symbol from the crow family, why not Cuchulainn 's raven?

Such might have expressed some of the criticism of the town's arms, some of it urged by well-wishers. But Mrs Chambers, with her Northern sectarian prejudices, was not a well-wisher. But generally her shafts at the three crows were not original. They were to be heard among the more bigoted of the local Protestants, the great majority of whom wanted to live in some kind of amity with the Catholics that greatly outnumbered them in the town. The less discreet sectarian commentators had it that the crows on the town's shield represented the Catholic priests and the power they exercised in the town. The crows had the shield to themselves; and the priests had the town much to themselves, or at least they dominated it.

Such was the sectarian sense in some of the local comments on the town's arms, at times uttered with little discretion, and sometimes in circles not usually seen in the town's taverns or other popular resorts. It had been noted that young bucks, come from the hunt to a shooting party in Lord Roden's demesne, when set on crows took aim with special venom. The rounds with the guns would be followed with an after-shoot garden' party, assembled under leafy canopies that drooped acorns and cones. At these functions, with Lord Roden and some of the county elite in attendance, Mrs Chambers, her hand petting the russet boa at her neck, might be heard to say that the three crows on the town's shield, thought so little about, even despised, by the town's quality, should be replaced by a trio of Lord Roden's squirrels.

The brown squirrels in the Roden demesne were a pampered lot. Even citizens with hatred or contempt for the town's greatest landlord were disposed to taking their leisure, when permitted, in his lordship's demesne, to watch his lordship's squirrels cavort in the well-wooded pastures. At our home in Clanbrassil Street we had no need to enter Roden's demesne to indulge or pamper his squirrels. As with the other houses on the West side of Clanbrassil Street, including the Northern Bank premises and Chambers' residence, the yard and garden at the back of our house ended at the great wall that guarded the Roden domain and kept without the town's commonalty.

At the bottom of our garden near the demesne wall we had a large beech tree, and in season it bore a rich crop of nuts. On the other side of the wall in the demesne trees of different species ranged in mass to obscure the further landscape. One of the trees near the wall extended its boughs to meet the branches of our beech tree; and in season some of the squirrels would come from the demesne on to our tree, foraging and frolicking in the higher branches, then gradually descending to lower levels and furtive familiarity with the garden scene. We sought to encourage this stage in the squirrels' incursions, and when we thought vainly to indulge their descent to the grass, with offerings of the more readily accessible fodder of bits of bread or cake, they rebuffed our approaches and took off to the branches. But even this retreat, with its many gymnastic turns was a delight to watch. Even at comparative rest and appearing seated, their paws nimbly engaged with nuts, the spritely creatures could enthral.

News of the squirrels' visits to our garden spread outside the family, and we had friends and acquaintances come to watch their antics in our beech tree. On one of these occasions the visitors were some women acquaintances of my mother's who were members of the Women's National Health Association. They came to watch the squirrels, but were soon joined by a number of other members of the Association and their friends. Having brought ready provisions along with them, the gathering turned out to be a garden party, apparently in aid of the Association. The affair must have been quite embarrassing for my mother, as my father, who, of course, would have been engaged in business at the time, had little love for some of the ladies at the head of the Association and less respect for Lord Roden and his squirrels.

One of our near neighbours, a member of the Women's Association, but with whom my mother had no contact, social or otherwise, was none other than Mrs Chambers, the bank manager's wife. They lived in the residence of the bank premises only four doors from us. From the back window of the upper floor in their residence she had been able to observe the squirrels' visits to our garden. Their gambols in our tree and descents to our garden had annoyed her, making her feel envious. She became resolved that by hook or by crook Lord Roden's squirrels would be induced to find sanctuary in her garden. Not in a mood to wait for seed or sapling to grow to fruit—bearing maturity, she would acquire a tree, a nut - or perhaps cone-bearing one, that would offer, she hoped, more welcome retreat or refuge to Lord Roden's itinerant squirrels. The storing season was now over, but by the spring she would have acquired her tree, with branches thrust forth to welcome their visitors and guests from the demesne.

There had been an eviction of a family from a middle-sized estate near the Water-works in Ravensdale, a wooded district a few miles from Dundalk. It had been the scene of demonstrations by the Evicted Tenants' Organisation. One of the creditors in the liquidation was the Northern Bank. Part of the estate was a stretch of wood, most of its trees matured, some of them of conifer varieties. To Mrs Chambers' order one of them with cones, it was said, that had special appeal to the squirrel species, was now uprooted and carted to the bank residence in Clanbrassil Street. In the darkness of an early spring morning an unusual hubbub awakened many of the other residents in the street, as the strange vehicle, an elongated forest-wagon bearing the tree, complete with roots, arrived near the bank. Commotion, signalled by a shattered shop window followed the arrival as the wagon and its load were being manoeuvred from the street through the gateway to the yard that flanked the bank premises. There followed more awkward operations with the wagon and its cargo as they were led through the yard and into the garden for the tree to have its roots deposited and staunched in a cavity prepared near the demesne wall. This part of the operation was the crucial one, since the sitting of the tree in its new habitat had to secure that some of its branches projecting over the demesne wall came in contact with branch or branches of trees there. All this was accomplished with the aid of practiced woodsmen, some of them having to be hoisted on to the demesne wall, and there, with ropes and pulleys, to help manoeuvre the tree to the vertical position. Now weeks were passing in the advance of spring. Mrs Chambers had been up in the mornings, watching her tree greet the sun, the invigorated boughs thrusting forth their cones, ranged as on candelabras waiting to be lit, their vigils shortening as the sun daily lengthened its arc rising from the horizon. With the birds in the demesne the nesting season was well advanced. Though with a few, late and perhaps more choosey home-builders, there was still foraging for nesting material in copse and hedge. But not with the demesne's crows; for those steeple-jacks of the woodlands had built earlier and at heights that kept their homes safe from marauder, leaving them free to disport themselves on branches at lower levels or on walls, with easy access to the ground.

In fact, some of them had perched themselves on the demesne wall, and a few had ventured on to Mrs Chambers' tree. Soon they were crowding on the tree, fiercely picking at the bark on the trunk and the branches, and it was not a casual visit, for they kept coming day after day. Their chorus of cawings sounded as paeans of thanksgiving or rejoicing. For Mrs Chambers it was an invasion of outrage. A superstitious woman, she was now regarding the crows' seizure of her tree as an act of vengeance for the many derogatory and contemptuous comments she had made on the species, particularly on the honoured status they had been given on the town's escutcheon.

If Mrs Chambers, a credulous, even superstitious woman, had had notions that some occult agency had been responsible for this visitation of the crows, she was soon to learn of more rational explanation. She had been visited by one of the Roden demesne gardeners, who at times had done some gardening work for the Chambers. He had seen from the demesne the descent of the crows on her tree, and suspecting the reason had ventured to investigate it. After examining the tree he found its bark was pitted with hardly visible holes. These bore the larvae, and in some cases the tiny mites, of insects, the perforations being mostly hidden by lichen, moss and other growths on the tree. The insects that had infested the tree were of a species the crows apparently found much to their taste.

To Mrs Chambers' anger was now added the suspicion that the Ravensdale lumber-men, more particularly the estate steward who had recommended the tree, had knowingly foisted on her an infected one likely when the season came to attract the demesne crows. She surmised those workmen now clearing the bankrupt Ravensdale estate were sympathetic with, if not, indeed, agents of the Evicted Tenants' Association.

Making notes of such events imagined in the Aldershot Prison cell, I suppose it was natural to conjure the watchmaker and jeweller, John McClure. His shop and business premises were directly opposite the Northern Bank in

Clanbrassil Street and had the shop window smashed when the vehicle conveying Mrs Chambers' tree was being turned from the street into the yard adjoining the Bank and part of its property.

John McClure, a member of the Dundalk Urban Council and of the Poor Law Board of Guardians, had done at least one spell in the custody of the law. And this was in circumstances that could be taken as demonstrating a fidelity to or integrity of trade which, one might have thought, should have greatly impressed the Templars, solicitous as they were for the good name of the trades, meaning the term not in the commercial but rather in the craft or manufacturing sense of the term.

McClure, a strong nationalist, had been suspected by the police of being a member of the I.R.B., the Irish Republican Brotherhood, a secret society organisation of the time that might be considered a bridging body between the Fenian Brotherhood and the emerging Sinn Féin organisation.

There had been a demonstration in the town commemorating the Manchester Martyrs. There had been some disorder and a few were arrested by the police. McClure was among them. Now McClure's competency in watch-making and repairing had had the modest beginning of his having learned the less complicated trade of lock-smith. No sooner was he lodged in a cell in the police barracks than he started manifesting his trade instincts by subjecting the elaborate lock of the cell door to critical examination. This was not at all, apparently, a search for defect in the lock that might facilitate escape. It was rather a search for lock rectitude, or rather for acceptable standards in locksmith competence. McClure found the mechanism was defective and that its apparent securing of the cell door could easily be undone.

Instead of taking advantage of this and planning his escape he reported it to the police charged with his custody; and furnished by them with tools to effect the necessary adjustments he effected the repairs, at the same time making effective his own incarceration. When some days later he was brought to court he was discharged by the magistrate on the plea of the police of his co-operation with them.

In time this performance of McClure when under custody in the police barracks was the subject of ridicule in the town. And the ridicule was scarcely less in The Temple where demonstrated respect for or devotion to one's trade was usually much esteemed but where conduct regarded as fatuous or else calculated to gain favours with the authorities was looked on with contempt. Still the ridicule following McClure's brush with the law seemed hardly to have affected his business and certainly not his activities on the public boards. He was still active both as a Town Councillor and Poor Law Guardian.

It was interesting to note how Christian amity or love was being promoted on the Town Council. The Municipal Councils throughout the country had replaced the old trade and merchant guilds which had functioned as local government organs for centuries but had been abolished with the enactment of the municipal reform legislation of the early 19th Century. Shortly after McClure's release from police custody he took to playing an active part in discussions in the Town Council on a proposal that the Council should procure itself a ceremonial mace, a likely expensive piece of workmanship of the gold-and-silver-smith's art, the contract for which would probably go to the McClure firm.

True, it was not Councillor McClure who made the mace proposal in the Council. Rather it was Councillor Cassidy, the leading merchant tailor in the town. In his speech the Councillor remarked on the drab and rural-like character of the Council's proceedings and public appearance. The work the Council was doing needed and deserved something of panoply or pageantry if only to arouse in the public a proper appreciation of the work.

When it came to what seemed a generally favourable reception of the proposal Councillor McClure felt urged to honour that principle of Council usage older even than the medieval guilds, which, put in common language declared: one good turn deserves another He pointed out that procuring themselves a mace would, going by tradition, imply that the Chairman of the Town Council would now have mayoral status; and this, of course, would mean that the mayor would have to be robed, as would, indeed, the Councillors themselves, and not forgetting the tip-staff who would handle the mace.

Councillor McClure could say much with his expressive eyes which he was now focussing in surveying critically his colleagues' lack-lustre wearing apparels. Some of his colleague Councillors had come there from their shop counters or offices. Some, like himself, had probably laid aside the tools of their trade to attend the Council meeting. Some might have on their Sunday suits, likely undistinguished three-piece hand-me-downs, a few in swallowtail coats. They would have doffed their hats for the Council meeting, and these, indeed, were the crowning pieces to their staid attire. The black hard hat, sometimes elongated to be a half tall one, seemed to be the standard head-dress of the Councillors, a quite undistinguished item of apparel, since nearly all adult males in the town seemed addicted to it. It seemed strange that men would crown themselves with this black casque, with its hard, sharp-edged brim that men violently disposed might use as a bird its ravenous beak, and which their women sought either to mock or atone for with their own more imaginative head dresses that current fashion decked with gay plumes and imitation flowers.

When the Council's debate on robing the Chairman and Councillors was proceeding it was seen that the Council robe would have to include appropriate head-dress. And here something of suitable design would have to be chosen, something, say, between the academic's and the ecclesiastic's head-dress. These were matters, to be sure, on which the Council would have to be advised by someone in the trade. At this point in the discussion Councillor McClure's attention was concentrated on Councillor Cassidy and perceiving the glow in that worthy's face he could read the Councillor's appreciation that a good turn had been rewarded with another good turn.

There followed a debate on the question of further appurtenances that might have to be acquired should the status of the Council be changed to mayoralty. It would only be proper that the mayor should be furnished with mayoral coach, with at least two horses, perhaps four. This extended the scope of interest in the proposal to further trades in the town, including coach-making and harness-making. If these trades were not directly represented on the Council, there likely would be auxiliaries there who would be mindful of the particular trades' interests. The spirit of the guilds survived.

Such would hardly be in the thoughts of the Councillors, who, even as they debated the mace and associated proposals, regarded themselves as public benefactors, actuated by the noble spirit of serving the people. Well, no decision was come to on the much debated proposal and sub proposals, when it was decided to adjourn further consideration of the matters. The Council was moved to this decision by recent pressure on the Councillors on the urgent need to do something about the slum problem in the town. The Public Health Officer had long been reporting outbreaks of fevers and the prevalence of other diseases in slum areas in the town, instancing particularly the insanitary hovels in such places as Shield's Yard, Wrightson's Lane and Squeeze-Gut Alley. The Board of Poor Law Guardians had reported on the inadequate facilities in the Fever Hospital, one of the Board's charges, to deal with the growing incidence of tuberculosis and the more frequently recurring fevers in the town and districts under the Board's jurisdiction. The Women's National Health Association had petitioned the Town Council on the urgency of doing something on the public health problems.

Some of the Councillors saw the situation as a re-housing problem, and the Council had been moved to make approaches to Lord Roden's agents, with a view of acquiring by purchase part of the Roden demesne as a housing site. Rumours had been circulating that the Earl was anxious to dispose of part of his estate which embraced much of the urban and district areas of the town.

Of course these matters had long been discussed in The Temple. Among the Templars were a few Town Councillors and Poor Law Guardians, as well as a few aspirants to those civic offices. It was not surprising, therefore, that Councillor and Poor Law Guardian McClure had become the subject of new ridicule among The Templars. It had become known he had taught his wife the secrets and practicalities of the watch-making and lock-smithing trades.

Mrs McClure had been seen in their shop with the probing eyepiece stuck in one of her eye sockets and held and manipulated there with what looked like high professional skill, as she directed delicate instruments in exploring the insides of a timepiece open before her. She seemed as assured at this as even a surgeon could be exploring the human anatomy.

The idea of disclosing, much less imparting, the skills of one's trade to a woman seemed to The Templars as something outlandish, something almost as unnatural as would be a woman's attempt to teach a man the mothering or labour maternity process that brought a child into the world.

There was much controversy in The Temple about the case. Mrs McClure had been seen in the act of repairing watches in their shop. It was also known Mrs McClure had been paying periodic visits to customers' homes servicing grandfather clocks and other large domestic time-pieces. Then there were the few public clocks, including the one in the Cathedral's new belfry. Looking after these, for which the firm had contracts, would, one would have thought, have entailed a certain amount of physical labour or manipulation which surely none but a savage would have regarded as suitable for a woman.

But even among The Templars there was surely one to plead that it was known John McClure's eyesight had been failing him for some time, a fact attested by his having taken to wearing thick-lensed spectacles. And in such circumstances it was likely he would have been anxious to pass his trade skills on to someone near him. The McClures had no children, and, being now apparently advanced in years, no prospects of such. So perhaps the choice for McClure had been, if he couldn't give his wife a child he'd give her his trade.

Or, perhaps it was her own assertion or initiative in the matter. Mrs McClure was an ardent feminist. She had espoused the cause of the local group that was supporting the Women's Suffrage Movement. Had she claimed initiation into the mysteries and practicalities of the lock-smithing and watch-making trades in assertion of the sex-equality principle? We are hardly likely ever to know. Nor is it likely anyone shall ever know the true reason why John McClure was willing to face ridicule by teaching his wife his trades, and why, earlier in his active republican days, whilst in police custody he willingly mended the lock of the cell door that was to keep him incarcerated.

We may wonder if it has been the impenetrability of the human that has driven some of the more intelligent of the race to try to comprehend what we call nature or outside phenomena, and thus has given us our great discoveries and inventions. Are we to regard the like of Aristotle, Galileo, Newton, Darwin, Edison, Marconi, Einstein as frustrated psychologists, unrewarded pryers into the human psyche, who turned to engage themselves on the less hidden secrets of the galaxies, the problems of gravitation, the origin of species, certain aspects of light and sound, etc.?

Chapter 5

I had got about this far in my notes or kind of shorthand on my reminiscences and my fancy's elaboration of them when the sound of footsteps approaching my cell warned me that danger might be near. I hastily concealed my notebook and pencil when suddenly the red-cap's key turned the lock in the door and the red-cap entered. He gave the order that I get ready for the draft. With the cell door open I could hear unusual activity going on apparently throughout the whole wing of the prison.

I proceeded to assemble the various parts of the infantryman's bag and baggage that had been allotted me and was in my charge since my entrance to the Glass-house Prison. These comprised the toilet and first-aid needs and the various other pieces of equipment that armies allot their foot soldiers. I loaded myself with the pack on my back and its webbing accessories girding my body, and waited for the cell door to be opened again. Soon it was opened, and two redcaps came into the cell. First they busied themselves with a search of the cell, apparently assuring themselves I was not walking off with any of His Majesty's property that I might have concealed in the pack I was now carrying.

If that was part of their mission I thought it superfluous as I expected that before being sent off on the draft we would be subjected to a thorough kit inspection. Even for much less important enterprises than assembly for draft the Glass-house prisoners were subjected to frequent kit inspections, often at unexpected times. It was usually done at squad or platoon drill when the prisoners would be ordered to unload the packs off their backs and lay the contents on the ground before them. If any of the prisoners' pockets seemed bulky they too would have to have their contents laid out.

When escorted to the parade ground I was fearful of search and discovery of my notebook and pencil, hidden in a cavity which, under my shirt and singlet, and with careful adjustments of muscles, I tried to maintain in the lumbar region of my body. The prison diet had helped this resource of finding hiding cavities in the body's outer recesses as well as experiencing the voids within. But there was no kit inspection this time. Those already assembled for the draft, numbering perhaps a hundred or more, were now marshalled in small groups and were being ordered to mount motor lorries waiting at the side of the parade ground.

I was escorted to one of the lorries at the end of the row. I was surprised to find there also under escort, a small group, among them some of the prisoners who had worked with me in the fatigue squad at the trench-digging on the shooting-range. Among them I recognised Lev and Gev, and the Welshman known as Taffy. There were a few others of that fatigue squad whose names I did not know or have since forgotten. We were ordered to mount the lorry, and, accompanied by some of the escort, we were driven off, coastwards. I was not sure whether our port for embarkation was Dover or Folkestone. We had been given no information as to our destination. At the time attempts were being made by the authorities to conceal the names of important ports and towns and places regarded as having strategic significance.

Contingents of troops from other areas were also arriving at the port, and when we were embarked on the large steamer, again anonymous, there seemed many hundreds of fully accoutred soldiers aboard. In the prison one of the anticipations that made the draft seem almost welcome to many of the prisoners was the belief that once embarked for service abroad you could regard yourself as free - that is, within the bounds of normal military service. Soon one freedom did seem apparent on the ship. You were free, if you had the money, to gorge yourself with buns and tea in the ship's canteen or sup in the ship's bar. Among the prisoner complement on the ship there would have been few to avail of the facility. The regulation was that from the moment you left the prison you had the status of a paid soldier, but, as the wage was paid weekly, its acquisition was still in front of us prisoners. But the ever-resourceful Lev had not to wait. He treated us to tea and buns and, evidently in forgiving mood, extended his hospitality to the three redcaps escorting us.

The escort kept us in a group more or less isolated from the others including the crew. Our main preoccupation was conjecture as to our destination. We got no enlightenment from the escort, but when bits of coastline started to appear on the horizon our general view was that we were bound for France. It was proving a rough crossing, and many aboard, including myself, were seasick. Eventually the coast loomed near enough for us to discern clear signs of a busy port. In the scramble to gather up and don equipment and move to the point of disembarkation we could hear talk that the port was Calais. Disembarked we re-assembled in our little group again to await instructions as to the next move. Meanwhile the troops were still leaving the ship and assembling at lorries along the docks. Eventually a lorry came towards us and the six of us were ordered on to it, the three redcaps joining us. We were still not given as much as a hint as to where we were going. We were soon out of Calais, and in about an hour we arrived in the town of Étaples, which, turned out to be the principal infantry base depot of the British forces in France.

We were driven to a military compound and lodged in a guardroom at the entrance. We were not put in cells, and were told we would soon be informed of what would be happening next. From the cap-badges and other insignia we saw about we learned we were at the headquarters of the Royal Army Service Corps. This eased our apprehensions somewhat. We had been speculating that our being isolated from the main body of the draft both in transit from the prison to the embarkation and on the channel crossing suggested we were still under surveillance and headed for some further spell of penal experience. To be now in the hands of the Royal Army Service Corps was somewhat reassuring. The Corps was made up of all kinds of specialist services which operated to serve the needs of what were called the fighting soldier units, the regiments that manned the battle lines. Included in the Service Corps were all kinds of craftsmen, engineers, bakers, carpenters and so forth.

We now felt better about the prospects ahead and waited with something like hope for further information. We were being called individually for perhaps questioning but more likely instructions. Those called did not return to the group. My turn came when I was escorted through passages to an apartment where an officer greeted me summarily with my rank, name and regimental number. These details he had certified in a folder, apparently containing my file, which lay on the table before him. Reading over the file he made an effort to be friendly. A young man with a strong Scottish accent, he had little of the stiff, Haw-haw manner of speaking which I had come to associate with the British military officers. I was to learn that this particular mark of the species was fast being modified and a new type of officer was being turned out with at least the outer traits more in accord with those of the ordinary people. This change, one supposed, was being brought about by the removal, in casualties, of many of the older type being replaced by new officers coming from the ranks now being reinforced by the operation of conscription.

The officer noticed in my file I had offered to work as baker. He questioned me as to my experience at the trade noting I had worked more at the confectionery than at the bread end of the trade. He told me it had been decided I should serve as a cook and not as a baker. As a cook I would have opportunity of showing whatever skill I had in cake-making. They were sending me on a three-weeks' course in a cookery school in Wimereux, a seaside place near Boulogne. The course would be in cookery for officers. I was to proceed by train to Boulogne that evening. During the few remaining hours I had in Étaples, which the British soldiers called Eataps, I was not to meet any of the Glass-house prison colleagues I had travelled with, so I learned nothing of how they had fared in their interviews. Some months later I was to meet one of them, Taffy, in a convalescent camp in the small French town of Bushy, an Army Medical Centre that was being crowded with the over-flow of casualties from Military hospitals.

I was now free, at least within the duties assigned me, and as I had a few hours in hand before getting the train for Boulogne I sauntered into Étaples town. Whatever attractions this small French town may have had in peace time, it had now little glamour or even identity. There were few of the town's folk to be seen, so many were the British soldiers afoot in the streets, either in small military formations proceeding on duties or in smaller groups spending off-duty recesses, gaping at windows or crowding into estaminets. There were those leaving the estaminets, some boisterous, some in song, their military bearing somewhat off the vertical from libations of French wine. There were scenes almost of carnival in the streets. This could seem like desperate efforts to forget the war that was going on only a few hours lorry ride from the town.

Around the centre of Étaples, there were lurid if, conforming with the reputed French taste, artistic signs of the war, in the posters appealing to local patriotism. They depicted some of the war excesses of the Bosch, the name now given the Germans, and pointed their alleged crimes in occupied France and Belgium, their outrages on women and children, their razing of homes and tabernacles. Even the larger poster, that of the Maid of Orleans, Joan of Arc, looked quite belligerent. She was depicted in shining armour, her breastplate protruding.

This could have prompted thoughts on how the art and artifices of war had changed. If any of the groups of tipsy or drunken soldiers passing in the street had stopped to look at the depicted Joan of Arc they would have turned to the poster their breasts girded, not with coats of armour, but with canvas satchels bearing their gas masks. In Joan's day the weapons of death and mutilation on the battlefield were of steel or other metal, often cumbrous in their handling. Now in war death or horrid injury to vital organs could come with the drawing of one's breath. All soldiers were now carrying the gasmask, and, as the enemy's poison gas was now being delivered in exploding shells and bombs, the mask was being held ready in areas far from the firing-lines and during off-duty recesses as well as on formal parades. Inside the satchel the gasmask was attached to a box of chemicals that filtered contamination from the air before being breathed through the mask.

Even individual soldiers or groups bound for the estaminet or other rendezvous of diversion carried the gasmasks at their chests. I had seen a queue of a dozen or so soldiers outside a premises which I took to be an unusually private-looking estaminet. For servicemen not on parade they looked unusually smartened-up, their buttons and insignia shining, that is so far as these were visible with the gas-mask satchels hanging on their breasts. I was to learn later that the premises was a brothel, a maison toléré, or licensed house of prostitution.

Thinking later of those soldiers in the queue, their breasts, even behind those hardly romantic-looking gas-mask satchels, probably pulsing to the anticipated joys of the brothel, one wondered what art of chemistry or other science could have been available to filter the spurious love to be purchased in such a place.

Of my brief stay of hours in Étaples this was one of the impressions that lingered long with me. Another was of a different kind, with its own significance. Wandering in the Étaples streets I heard sounds of music coming from not far-off. I followed the sounds to their source, another army compound of huts and more permanent looking timber structures.

The sounds, mostly from singing and playing of a piano and other instruments, were coming from something like an entertainment hall. Posters at the entrance announced an entertainment by a concert party come from London. I was to learn that such concert parties of professional entertainers made regular visits to France and other war areas to entertain the troops during their rests or recesses from the firing lines. The entertainment provided by the concert parties was usually of the music-hall variety type. Light vocalists and comedians predominated.

Still on the street I listened to some of the concert. It included some of the vocal favourites then current, such as *Keep the Home-fires burning*, *It's a long way to Tipperary*, and *Bring me back to Blighty*, a more sophisticated sentimental number was *Roses of Picardy*. Perhaps the ditty that evoked the loudest chorus and applause was *Pack up your troubles in your old kit-bag, and smile, smile, smile*.

Whether any of such songs ever inspired a British soldier to deeds of martial ardour, I'll never know. They bored me, and made me depressed to think that the like could entertain soldiers claimed to be fighting for superior cultural values and their predominance over the barbarism of German Kultur.

I was glad to turn from the compound and give ear to sounds coming from the opposite side of the street. They came from what looked like a large private residence, and the sounds were of a piano. The notes went in short phrases that were often repeated before a new phrase or cadence was started. The pianist was obviously rehearsing; and the clarity and expression put into the fingering made me feel that both the player and the composer of the piece were of high calibre, he, or she, played the runs of the main themes so often I was able to memorise some of them, particularly in the slow movement. Later I came to learn the piece was Beethoven's *Pathétique* Sonata.

That experience in an Étaples Street was to remain vivid with me for a long time, not only from the depth and nobility of the music but from the thought that in this small French town, with its hoardings blaring hatred of Germany, there was at least one musician, and presumably appreciative hearers who could, at least momentarily forget the war to listen to the music of one of whom the Germans boasted as being one of their great geniuses.

In the Cookery School discipline as exercised by the teachers and other staff had its own irksomeness. For this they had the same motive that kept the Keepers in the Glasshouse on their metal, the knowledge that their safe jobs away from the firing lines could well be in jeopardy should laxity in exerting discipline be proven against them.

Outside the time given to the classes in the school there was little in the way of military duties to occupy the students. As in Étaples the main recourses for relieving the boredom of military life in Wimireux was the estaminet or the brothel, the latter to be availed of in Boulogne. I was little attracted to either distraction. Neither the French wine nor French beer appealed to me, and the coffee available in the estaminets was of a war brew hardly more attractive. However, I was prepared to sup them in small potions, as an excuse for visiting an estaminet near the school, the real purpose of my visit being to try out my French on some of the locals.

I had a rather shaky basis in the language. At school I had done about a year in its study when I left. I had liked the language; but the school study had been more literary than vocal. The Christian Brother who taught us had not acquired anything like the proper French phonetics. As to the subject matter of his lessons, this was much influenced by the religious vocation he had brought to the teaching profession. We were taught about the Little Flower and the pilgrimages to Lourdes. After my leaving the Brothers' School my father had taught me something about secular France, about Voltaire and the 1789 Revolution.

I wanted to learn more about the period, even about the French Kings, their wives and their mistresses, the courtiers whose extravagances had fostered the age of elegance. The Burbon royalty seemed not so insufferable a lot of bores as their contemporary British royalty. I wanted to hear something of French speech retold, something of the causeries in the salons or the rhetoric in the Directory that sped the tumbrills to the guillotine.

With much hesitation I ventured my French on some of the natives in a few visits to the estaminet. I did not get very far, mainly for their difficulties in understanding my French. As well, they showed little interest in discussing the old French royalty, or the like of Voltaire, or Danton, or even Napoleon.

They were preoccupied more with current affairs and events. They had already suffered losses in the war, in dear ones killed or wounded, in relatives and friends made refugees from homes seized or destroyed in enemy action. Then there were the ever attendant worries of domestic shortages and the prospects of the situation worsening. Over all this apparent discouragement of my efforts to talk bad French on subjects they evidently thought remote or irrelevant was the feeling that the idea being fostered by British propaganda that the British troops were in France to defend that country, or wrest its occupied parts from its enemies, was one hardly given credence by the French themselves. It was soon apparent there was little feeling of comradeship between the British soldiers and the French people encountered, and in the estaminets and cafés there seemed little likelihood of the wine or beer, and much less the coffee, promoting it.

As an alternative to the unpromising attraction of the estaminet, there was the allurement of the brothel. My primary reaction to it was of fear, not only of its likely reward of unfulfilment, but rather of its travesty of or disillusionment from earlier teaching. I had been brought up with the notion that in sex relations man was the pursuer, even the aggressor, that woman was the pursued, often the reluctant partner, even victim. Here the woman was parading herself, faking initiative, and getting paid for the dissimulation.

It took later years to learn there are no such clear-cut distinctions as pursuer and pursued distinguishing the sexes one from the other, that in individual cases it may be one or other of the sexes takes the initiative, and probably in many cases both. It was in this last relationship I came to see the sex ideal to be followed; and, of course, this ruled out such adjustment being secured by bribe or payment.

With such reflections on the estaminet and the brothel I came more and more to pass the evenings of my days in the cookery school with my notebook in the seclusion of my hut. I had been issued with a most official looking stamped envelope and some sheets of writing paper with permission to write home. Such writing material was issued as rations periodically to all servicemen in war theatres. You were warned that your letters would be subject to censoring. I wrote my first letter to my mother and father since my imprisonment about six months before. I enclosed a note for my Aunt Mary, knowing her concern about me was likely to be as worrisome as that of my parents. Writing to them put me in reminiscent mood, and I had recourse to the notebook.

My Aunt Mary, my mother's sister, had been a second mother to me, her arms a ready refuge when fear or shame made me flee the less indulgent embraces of my mother. Indeed, as I grew in adolescence my mother's arms seemed raised to me more in monitory signals than as anything like welcome from my widening quests beyond the home. Both my parents must have noticed my increasing absences after school hours when more and more of my time was being given to escapade in conjectured haunts in the town with certain school chums. These distractions had begun encroaching on the times normally given to my school homework in the afternoons and evenings. As to my obligations here my parents were equally vigilant. My mother, therefore, had no difficulty in persuading my father to buy me a tricycle. These were becoming popular with the children of townsfolk that could afford them. The tricycle, to be ridden within the confines of our yard, would serve to keep me at home and thus at hand for the school homework. I am not sure as to what time in our lives conscience first starts troubling us; and am content to leave research or pursuit of the trouble-raising ogre to the psychologists or with those ridden with so intolerable feelings of guilt they entertain plans of laying the monster. I should imagine it starts rearing its head around the time we begin suspecting people of ulterior motives.

I know my mother was, for her own motives, as keen about the progress of my education as was my father, for his philosophical reasons. But I came to suspect that my mother had another reason for getting me the tricycle. Our yard, where I was to ride it covered a long and wide area, running from the front gate to our home to the hedges dividing the yard from the garden. It went down the full length of the house and two large out-houses beyond. The yard's surface was of earth, pitted here and there with holes made by the scratchings of Aunt Mary's poultry, which had the run of the yard.

I had not made many runs on my tricycle when it became evident the action of the wheels was extending these ruts on the yard's surface. I suppose it was my neophyte enthusiasm with the new machine was mainly responsible for transforming the yard into an area of small craters with surrounds of pebbles that were likely to catapult to walls and windows when charged over by the tricycle. On wet days the pits in our yard were filled with water; but, wet or dry, the scene in the yard presented anything but an inviting sight to anyone visiting our home.

Long before the advent of the tricycle I should have noticed my mother's disgust, often anger, about the presence of her sister's poultry in the yard. True, the poultry-shed or hen-house was at the very bottom of the yard near the garden. It was quite commodious, having been converted from a former coach-house and stables. But, once out-of-doors, the birds took the run of the yard. At the sign of rain, or perhaps from strong sun, they tended to gather at the top of the yard under the awning of the conservatory at our hall-door. This portal was an opulent one of dark mahogany with brass mountings; and above, behind the curved glass panels, the multi-coloured geraniums and tropical plants. For my mother it must have had the hallowness of an altar. And for my aunt's hens to gather there to preen and cackle, and for the cockerel to prate there his insolence, would surely seem an intolerable affront to any respected caller.

There was only one thing now to be done with the wretched yard, and, as my mother was the arbiter in such things, she saw to it that it was done. The yard from top to bottom was given a surface of concrete. The head yard-man in the premises up the street, where our bread-vans and horses were stabled, undertook the work, and, as well, arranged for the poultry to be transferred to the upper or bakery yard where they would have the run of the stables, and where incidentally they could be maintained at less cost than when under Aunt Mary's care. It turned out, of course, that the yardman served his own interests in the change.

Though she paid them odd visits in their new, and, indeed, more suitable home, the transfer of Aunt Mary's poultry from the yard of our home was something she felt very much, and that I felt to some extent on my conscience, but, on reflection, more assignable to my mother's.

As will already have been conjectured there was at the time a sharp social divide in our home. Following their marriage my aunt and her husband, whom I had come to know as my Uncle John, were given accommodation with us pending their securing a home for themselves. As it turned out their stay with us lasted several years and thus embraced the time of my infancy and some of my school years. They were to have no family of their own, and this led to their fostering me almost as an adopted son. My mother, though showing all due signs of affection for me, accepted this fostering, perhaps for its leaving her more time for the social activities and interests which occupied her and which neither my aunt nor uncle shared.

It was not that these social activities took my mother much out of our home. My father's many social contacts ensured quite a regular round of social occasions in our home, alternating from the more intimate and often more or less spontaneous get-togethers in our sitting room to the more formal gatherings upstairs in our drawing room. It was in the former apartment, the sitting room, with its easy access from our hall-door and, on the other side, its ready communication with the kitchen, that the really sociable occasions occurred. To be described primarily as my parents' living room, where they ate and supped and entertained their more intimate friends, the sitting room was larger and more suitable for social entertainment than the drawing room above. It was appropriately equipped in that its most conspicuous article of furniture was the mahogany piano, and this was matched with chairs and divans that still left enough room for a large table which in turn could be pushed aside to leave room for dancing, at least for a few couples, should the social turn of events so determine. The only other conspicuous piece of furniture in the apartment was the bookcase. This was purely a decorative piece of mahogany furniture, for its contents of large imposing-looking volumes in no way represented my parents' tastes in reading matter. They were made up of a series of encyclopaedias, some bound volumes of the *Illustrated London News* and, on the bottom shelf, the *Lives of the Saints*. This last work, sumptuously bound in green covers and embossed in gilt, represented the only tomes in the book-case that had now any currency or call in the sitting-room. And that call was limited to my mother's jewellery requirements. These could change from day to day and even within the day. My mother kept her brooches and other adornments in those volumes of the *Lives of the Saints*. How she apportioned them to the respective saints and called on them to protect her rarities was a matter, I suppose, that lay deep in my mother's theology. Our family reading matter was to be seen more in my parents bedroom, above the sitting room, where my father had his private library.

My Aunt Mary and Uncle John rarely came to our sitting room, still less to the drawing room. They were content to live mostly at the back of the house, in the kitchen and, above that, in their bedroom, an apartment that had its holy arbor in the altar of statues and holy pictures in a corner of the room, draped with scarlet hangings and dimly-lit with the ever-burning Sacred Heart lamp.

John Cooper, who was of small farmer stock, was a man of simple tastes, in accord generally with those of his wife. They shared neither my mother's social interests or ambitions, nor my father's more serious intellectual and cultural pursuits. Cooper's association with my father was largely a matter of trade and the exigencies of a trade dispute. Each of the families lived largely to themselves in their respective parts of the house, with myself and the servant or maid for the time being as a kind of liaison between the families.

The distinction was seen in the class of callers coming to the house. Most of my parents' callers came to the hall door, those for the Coopers went down the yard to the back door. Perhaps the distinction was best seen in the kind of beggars that called. In Dundalk and in other urban areas generally at the time mendicancy was much a way of life. There was the large number of beggars who tried to take the bad or humiliating look out of mendicancy by turning it to a performance by voice or instrument or feat of bodily contortion or distortion proffered as public entertainment on the town's streets. Then there were the many who made regular calls at business premises and private residences, making direct appeals for alms, and hopeful the response will be in cash rather than in kind.

The local authority, the Urban Council and the Poor Law Guardians were ever much concerned with the local mendicancy. The Poor Law Guardians were responsible for the administration of the Poor Laws locally, including the running of the Poor House and the issuing of Out-door Relief vouchers to the deserving poor. This latter measure took the form of entitlement to parcels of provisions on presentation of vouchers at authorised grocers, and was intended as a cheaper way of relieving the necessitous than maintaining them in the Poor House. Besides, many of the needy preferred the Out-door Relief, stringent though it was, to the stigma and constraint of being incarcerated in the Poor House. The Poor House was known also as the Work House. Under the British Poor Laws the institution of the Poor House was conceived as being as self-supporting as was possible, so that with the operation of manufacturing work of many kinds within the institution it could be regarded as more or less self-maintaining, and thus not a burden on the tax-payers or rate-payers.

The rate-payers in the town were of the business and property owning classes, and the Town Councillors and Poor Law Guardians who had the responsibility of determining and collecting the rates were drawn almost wholly from those classes.

It was, therefore, to be expected the Councillors and Guardians would want to keep the town rates, including those for the up-keep of the poor, as low as possible. One of my mother's uncles was a Town Councillor and Poor Law Guardian. Michael Deane was a successful publican in the lower end of the town. He had long service on the public boards, and was well acquainted with the town's mendicants and their problems. He was a conscientious Guardian in that he was ever concerned in seeing that as few mendicants as possible should resort either to the provision of Out-door Relief or being a charge on the Poor House. He thus encouraged people, friends and acquaintances, to support the itinerant beggars that would call at their places of business or their homes.

This, as my father put it, amounted to something like a campaign for the adoption of mendicants as regular callers at the residences of the charitable. The Church was giving spiritual voice to the Guardian's concern that the better-off citizens play their part in relieving the destitute. The theme in this year's Lenten retreats in the parish was Charity, the congregations being exhorted to give all they could afford to the poor. With such clamour for support of the mendicants, and with their numbers swollen, again, as my father expressed it, one had to be careful in the choice of one's beggar.

Perhaps the social division in our home was best shown in the classes of beggars that called respectively at the back door and the hall door. At the back door, where my Aunt Mary was hostess, the callers, apart from tradesmen or messengers, were usually of the recognisably destitute kind, some itinerant performers, others openly begging. Mostly, if not all, they would be cases recommended by the Uncle Micky for support or adoption by my Aunt. She was his favourite niece and, unlike my mother, much disposed to meeting his wishes. Sometimes the caller was admitted to the kitchen and served a meal as well as given alms usually in the form of cash. An example was the regular who came at least once weekly, the Clappers Byrne. He, always raggedly dressed, seemed with just enough youth in him to execute a kind of dervish dance on the bottom step at the back-door, the while playing a mouth-organ held in one hand, the other engaged wielding bone clappers in time to the music.

The Clappers had learned to call and perform when there was a meal going in the kitchen, when, following his performance a knock on the back door gained him entry to the kitchen and a seat at the table. As regards the kitchen help or servant, sometimes called a maid, it should be explained that this kind of domestic female assistant was in common usage or service at the time. Usually they were young women from families of small farmers or labourers living in rural areas not far from the town. They were engaged at the hiring fair, an annual market-like event that was held in the town when the young women to be offered for domestic service were brought to town by the parent or guardian and stood in the market-place to be haggled over by prospective hirers. If I remember rightly in my time in the town the hiring price for a servant was twenty pounds (£20) a year, with board and lodging.

In our home domestic help did not come from the hiring fair, but from families of employees in our bakery. Usually we had one domestic help, sometimes two, when perhaps the sister of the one was brought in as a nursemaid or to help on special occasions. Regarding these domestic helps generally and the people that employed them, the shopkeepers and others of the middle-classes in the town, I think it could be claimed there was little class distinction evidenced, the domestic or servant being regarded at least to some extend as part of the family. With the upper or what was called the gentry class it was different. There the servants were kept very much in their places.

Certainly my Aunt Mary felt no lowering of status in working and dining with our domestic help in our kitchen, or in having at table the performing mendicant, the Clappers Byrne. With the kitchen help, or servant, and herself at the table accompanying their beggar at their meal, no doubt my aunt regarded this as an appropriate way of meeting the requirements of the Uncle

Micky and the injunctions of the Lenten missioners. As for the mendicant in his bedraggled and ill-fitting clothes, he did not seem that much out of place with my aunt and the domestic help, the former in her black, full-sleeved and full-and-long-skirted costume, modelled almost like a nun's, and the latter's less voluminous imitation of the model in grey.

Contrasting with all that was my mother's life style. This was to be seen at once in the way she dressed and in the people she chose to be callers at our hall-door. My mother did not go out much, and, not being greatly disposed to reading, much of her time at home was given to vigilance. She had regular times for expecting callers at the hall-door, when she would wait in the nearby sitting-room, and then, mostly in the late afternoon, she would run up to the drawing-room, again on a mission of vigil, to watch at one of the long windows running almost from ceiling to floor and draped its full length with lace hangings.

What an amenity - I should say invention - was the lace curtain. In the main thoroughfare of Dundalk, Clanbrassil Street, on both its sides the buildings were residences as well as business premises. Above the ground floors that served as shops, or stores, or offices, or consulting-rooms would likely be drawing-rooms or sitting-rooms, whence the residents at intervals from their businesses would survey the street below where people passed on foot, some to gape at shop windows, some scampering on the road-way as carriage or hackney-car made its way through the thoroughfare.

In their own way these curtained drawing rooms or sitting rooms were grandstands or theatre-boxes where the residents ensconced themselves to be spectators of what was going on in the street. Those passing in the street, even among them the mendicants that called at doors, were important for these ensconced burgers who were making their living in a sense valeting to these assorted pedestrians, furnishing them their clothes, their comestibles and other material wants, though the trading burgers would scorn such description of their services.

My grandmother was at an age when she had become largely an observer of life, life seen as a fast-changing kaleidoscope refracted through the weft and woof of a lace curtain. On days of the week, when her mood or the turn of the weather urged her, she would be assisted by the domestic help from her bedroom along the short corridor to the drawing room. There she would be seated and made comfortable before her favourite window, with the curtain suitably adjusted in front of her, lest its clinging folds should balk her fading sight.

Sometimes the street, like a theatre, had special spectacles that could be anticipated and therefore could be regarded as calling on the spectator or audience for special observance. Thus, on Saint Patrick's Day, and on a few other stated occasions in the year when bands and banners made spectacle in the thoroughfare, my grandmother was less disposed to be hid or veiled by the lace hangings and was to be seen from the street sitting in state arranged in the most formal of her white lace bonnets and the most sumptuous of her black lace shawls.

A similar observance by her was likely on the occasions when public display and ceremony was accorded Cardinal Logue or other high ecclesiastic, or some noteworthy political leader. In between these special occasions there were still enough happenings throughout the year in Clanbrassil Street to lure my grandmother to her recognised post at the drawing-room window. There were the itinerant musicians who had long marked her as a reliable patron and had well marked the pitch on the street whence she was to be saluted or serenaded by performer in sure anticipation of reward. The most frequent performers among these were the tambourine-player with the bear and the organ-grinder with the monkey. These two performers were separate or independent artists, and were at pains to come at different times and not to appear associated with one another.

The tambourine-man's performance was the simple one of beating his instrument to keep time with the bear's dancing from one hind-leg to the other. The organ-grinder's performance was even simpler. He just kept turning a handle attached to the music box that had a stump underneath supporting it on the ground. The monkey sat on the box, extending a begging hand to the passers-by. Both the tambourine-player and the organ-grinder had been coming long enough to the well-defined pitch on the road-way to have become well acquainted with the comings and goings of my grandmother in the drawing-room above.

Usually she was well prepared for their visits and for what had become something like command performances. She had a daily supply of cakes from our bakery, her favourites being in the small varieties of Paris buns and the like. When the bear and its accompanist had finished their performance she would have the window raised and a few buns cast to the bear. This would be followed by a more resonant offer to the accompanist when coppers would fall on the pavement to round-off his coda with a happy jingle. The organ-player and his monkey likewise had had their reward in the jingle of her pennies on the curb.

I don't know if my grandmother was a lover of horses. In those days Clanbrassil Street, as indeed, most of the other streets, was seldom seen without them. As yet the motor-car was seen only as an occasional oddity, when some eccentric, maybe a retired army officer or Castle official, made a foray into the streets in a contrivance that tugged and spluttered like a boat caught in shallow waters.

Special occasions for horses in the streets were the parades that heralded the opening of the circus in the town. In these the horses shared the honours with other quadrupeds such as elephants and camels and the wild animals exhibited in cages, with their attendant escorts of clowns and acrobats.

Other occasions, and more exclusive ones, for horses in the streets were, of course, the weddings of well-to-do couples when their carriages, often open for display of nuptial styles, were drawn leisurely through the main thoroughfare by show horses as well-groomed and styled.

Then there was the annual three-days race meeting outside the town when horse-vehicles of all kinds made continuous procession through the streets to and from the Kilcurry racecourse. More frequent than this event were the cattle and sheep sales held in the Fair Green on the Castletown River edge of the town. This event, held every month, brought the bizarre feature, the parade of the stallions. The stallions, come to town for the fair-days, were advertised in the newspapers, with particulars of their pedigrees, their place of lodging in the town, and the times their services were available. Their parade through the streets was quite a sight. A groom attempted to lead or rather grapple with each of the stallions, as the beast, its muscles taut and flaunting, its mane gaily be-ribboned, pranced its way through the streets to the merchant's yard with the stabling to be the stallion's domicile for its stay in the town. One of the stallions was stabled in Dearey's Yard, adjoining the firm's provision stores. At the time I was at school with one of the Dearey boys, apparently one determined to be a pioneer in sex education and with something of the business initiative of his father. To be surreptitious witnesses or spectators at the stallions working sessions, he smuggled a few of his school chums, including myself, into a boarded-up part of the yard where, through chinks in the boards, we were able to have glimpses of the stallion in service. He, our school chum, charged us a penny each for this elementary - and, shall we say, spectacular? - lesson in sex education. I suppose it was cheap in a rare market, considering the like was hardly to be had at any price in the Christian Brothers' curriculum.

Chapter 6

My mother's visits to the drawing room and her vigils at her favourite window and curtain were more urgent and discriminating than my grandmother's. Her reconnoitring was made through a finer, but not less revealing mesh of the lace hangings, for the need felt for concealment was greater than that felt in the case of her mother-in-law's, my grandmother's, vigils. Right opposite our home was the premises of Backhouse, one of the principal general merchants in the town.

The Backhouses, like nearly all who ran businesses in Clanbrassil Street, or, indeed, in other parts of the town, still had their residences or homes, on or above their business premises. This was still at a time before trades-people became ashamed of their trades and sought refuge from the like in secluded villas or other distant apartments. It was before some of the bigger merchants started flight to a new suburb, a collection of red-brick houses called the Crescent. The site was near the County Jail; and perhaps for some of the flitting merchants it represented a vestigial call to proximity with home more appropriate, or perhaps just a flight from conscience.

Mrs Backhouse was one of the leaders of fashion in the town. Her side of the street opposite ours had the sun in the afternoons when, weather permitting, she was want to stroll towards the south end of the street, her toilette the admiration or envy of many staring on the way. She would probably be on her way to a meeting of the Women's National Health Association or some high social function, but the while ever mindful that in their home her husband had but to run down the stairs from their bedroom or sitting-room to be busy at his counter or at checking the accounts in the office. The same could be said of Mrs. Chambers, the wife of the Northern Bank manager. She, another lady of fashion, though living a few doors down on our side of the street, on bright days in the afternoon took to the other side, to disport her figure in leisurely promenade. She, too, would likely be headed for meeting or function, and again, like Mrs. Backhouse, would probably be mindful of return to a home where her husband, the Bank Manager, had his workplace.

My mother was not a member of any of the town's societies or organisations. Her social life was satisfied largely in entertaining those my father brought to our home and in odd visits she paid her friends in different parts of the town. Outside of these activities she was largely a watcher of the social scene. Hence her vigils at the windows in the drawing room. She would be curious to observe Mrs Backhouse's or Mrs Chamber's new hat, whether fashion had decreed the bird's wings to be mono - or multi-coloured, or whether they be splayed on the hat's brim or raised to the crown. Apart from the current materials and cuts of costumes and skirts, there were the styles of the important accessories at the time, the neck-and hand-muffs, and whether they be of feather, flounce or astrakhan.

My mother had a discerning eye for all these vagaries of fashion and was eager to adapt or adjust them from the best walking models to be seen in the street, and within the competence saved after meeting the household expenses. Though my mother, like her sisters, was a little below middle height, her erect carriage and poise of head made her seem taller, a figure that could display current modes.

It was this fastidiousness in dress and manner that expressed best the care she exercised in choosing her favourite beggars. Of these Miss Julia Cole was the peer or peeress. A spinster of around my mother's age, and of like deportment and tastes, Julia Cole had retained her title to be addressed as Miss, a dignity rarely conceded to beggars. Perhaps it was significant that Julia begged only in Clanbrassil Street, or rather in a small circle of Clanbrassilers who worked successfully and lived in a thoroughfare that had got its name from an old family of aristocrats, and who were now tenants of that family's successor, the Earl of Roden. I myself was a born Clanbrassiler, begot in bedroom above the family bakery and shop. On my ablutions for baptism breathed the incense of bread baking in the oven below and the odour of bakehouse perspiration. I was to grow up with the impression that this close world of the Clanbrassilers, this living with work bred something like compassion or tendency to the best social virtues. I thought it opened hospitable doors, and that no one in the town was to be more welcomed or honoured than he or she reputed to have come down in the world, the sedate but humble-seeming person said to have seen better days.

Miss Julia Cole, my mother's favourite beggar, was such a person, though as to the better days from which she had come down there was recurrent speculation in the town. With fitting deportment she could seat herself at the piano in our sitting room and discourse excerpts from the best music in sensitive style. Probably alone among our visitors, or sharing the privilege with the family doctor, this visitor was given access to my parents bedroom. Her interest there was my mother's wardrobe or wardrobes, from which Miss Julia Cole appeared to have the right of choice to make her own. She herself was always well dressed, and when she arrived at our home her progress to the bedroom was something like a fashion model's parade.

She would beckon my mother's attention to the grand, almost new costume or cloak or other substantial piece of wearing apparel she had on her, intimating it was a gift from the wardrobe of kind Mrs Backhouse. On other visits she would mention the source of her current toilette as the wardrobe of her friend Mrs Chambers or some other charitable lady of fashion in the town. It was to be presumed that when my mother parted with some piece of apparel from her wardrobe to Julia the latter would parade it before her other benefactresses, drawing their attention to the gift her friend Mrs Swift had given her from her wardrobe. It was easy to see such traffic was likely to incite competition among these ladies to outdo one another in the scope of their benevolence. Is inherent even in charity or philanthropy, that urge to seem superior or dominant which is the motor of competition?

The cynic might say women are ever rivals, even when they dispense charity, for them a virtue to be dispensed from excess of wardrobe or cupboard, but rarely from the soul, reluctantly from the tongue. The more thorough cynic might add: are men any better?

At length it became noticed in the street that Julia's displays of her toilettes were subject to such frequent changes, and questions were being asked as to what she was doing with her cast-offs. Then it began to be bruited she was disposing of them to a cousin of hers who kept a second-hand clothes shop in Drogheda. When this was confirmed it was to have a chilling effect on some of her donors or benefactresses. Apparently they did not like the idea of their philanthropy being sullied by commerce. It was enough having their husbands all day at trade and carrying its audits to bed with them at night.

I got to know Julia in the early days of her visits. She was always well attired, and if the clothes were sometimes ill-fitting, they still had the aura or stamp of the town's haute monde. She performed various, often secret commissions for her benefactors, or benefactresses. For my mother and a few other residents in Clanbrassil Street she rendered the service of escorting their children to the kindergarten school, called the Grande School, of the Sisters of Mercy Convent in an east suburb of the town, and calling there in the afternoons and returning us to our homes. In some cases this occurred irregularly when the servant or nursemaid in the particular house was not at hand to perform the service. Julia usually had three or four children to look after. I was one of the constant ones in the group, not because of the unavailability of our servant but to my mother's giving way to my sometimes noisy preference for Julia rather than the servant Mini as my escort.

Julia treated her charges in the most motherly way, always having on her person quantities of assorted sweets, which on the way to and from school she awarded us as we answered her queries as to how we were discharging our duties at school and at home.

And now that Julia Cole had fallen on lean days with her patrons and had all but discontinued her calls in Clanbrassil Street, there was much less talk about her, unless perhaps in that establishment of abiding town lore, The Temple. In her more prosperous days she had been a fairly frequent visitor there, to it's Gobi snug, of course, for unless on very rare occasions, women were not admitted to the Grande Snug. Julia liked her glass of port, and in the less stilted or less academic atmosphere of the Gobi snug she was able to find in some of the regulars more congenial company. The reporter and archivist of a kind, Pat Byrne, had had much conversation with her there.

Byrne had become quite a genealogist with, among other projects of research, commissions from visiting Americans of Irish ancestry to look up their pedigrees, hoping the family tree would be found to go back to some such link as Brian Boru or Duns Scotus. He became interested in Julia Cole and her antecedents. It might be better to start this brief account of Byrne's researches on the subject with a summary of what he found out about Julia Cole's mother, Julia Moody.

She had come of small farmer stock in a district near Newry, about eight miles north of Dundalk. She had been orphaned at early age, and had been brought up in a Sisters of Mercy Orphanage. She was trained there as a seamstress and when come of age she was given the chance of employment in a clothing workshop in Newry. At the same time she had heard of a job as parlour maid or servant in the household of one of the landed gentry, the estate being nearer Dundalk on the road between Newry and that town. The owner of the estate was Brigadier Caden-Cole, a retired officer of a cavalry regiment in the British Army.

The Brigadier had served in the Crimean War, and had been wounded in the battle of Balaclava, an engagement immortalised in Tennyson's poem *The Charge of the Light Brigade*. The estate, comprising several hundred acres and a large modernised residence, had been previously owned by a line of ancestors. The Brigadier's army service before the Crimean campaign included spells in India and in the African Continent. He had no family or relatives that were known. A bachelor well in middle life, he liked entertaining congenial friends or associates, and kept a fairly large domestic staff.

Young Julia Moody apparently thought there could be more glamour in being a member of the Brigadier's domestic staff than in toiling as a seamstress in a Newry factory. The Brigadier's residence had the name of The Alma, the name having been chosen by himself, for it was in the Crimean battle of that title that Caden-Cole had won his highest military distinction.

After Julia Moody had taken up her post as parlour-maid in Caden-Cole's establishment, she began spending some of her time-off with friends in Dundalk. Among them it appears she had a special friend in the person of a youth of the name of James Fagan. The youth worked in the bottling stores of the leading liquor supplier and groceries establishment in the town, Messrs Backhouse.

In his spare time Fagan did some bottling work for Mr Conlon, the proprietor of The Temple tavern. In that establishment Fagan had tried to launch himself as an amateur entertainer, with rather reluctant audiences' response to his not considerable vocal and histrionic talents. As a result The Templars conferred him with a nickname intended to emphasise his truer and more likely, more abiding talents. They nicknamed him The Bottler Fagan.

It seems he was now faring no better in his attentions to Julia Moody. She had cooled-off in the rather desultory courtship, in which he had been cast in the more ardent role. Their acquaintances were not surprised at the way the courtship had gone. They thought that Julia Moody, now a buxom and handsome young woman of rather vivacious temperament, was likely to attract a more presentable and better positioned suitor than the rather common-place labourer who evidently couldn't rise to any better position in Backhouse's stores.

Then, suddenly, Julia Moody was no longer to be seen in Dundalk, or, indeed in The Alma estate. There was good reason for this, as was known to a few who were more or less directly concerned. Julia Moody was in a private nursing home in Dublin, there being delivered of a child, the love child of Brigadier Caden-Cole. The Brigadier had privately arranged for the accouchement and the later fosterage of the child. But the mother died at the birth, and the later christening of the infant, a girl, came to be performed by the Rev. Father Crilly, who had come specially from Dundalk, where he held the post of spiritual director of the town's Poor House and Fever Hospital.

In that office Father Crilly had had much experience concerned with illegitimate children born in the institution of the Poor House. How he came to hear of Julia Moody's being sent to the Dublin nursing home was not unearthed in the research. It certainly wasn't from the secretive Brigadier. Father Crilly could hardly have been regarded as a friend of his. Indeed, it was quite the contrary, the clergyman regarding the retired British Army-man as alien in creed and political and social associations. These facts were very much in the priest's mind when, on the mother's death, he performed the christening ceremony in the nursing home. He gave the child its first name Julia, after the mother, and the surname Cole, after the father, Brigadier Caden-Cole. Father Crilly's choice of the surname was perhaps to bring home to the Brigadier the responsibilities of paternity.

Journalist Byrne's researches on the Brigadier and The Alma brought further lore for discussion in The Temple. It appears that Caden-Cole, though keeping much to himself on his estate, entertained occasionally, when he would have company, usually of the military kind. There was a military barracks in Dundalk, an establishment well provided with stables, for its occupants were always of the cavalry kind, sometimes a regiment of huzzars, at other times lancers.

On this occasion the Brigadier, now well in his seventies, was entertaining a group of huzzar officers from the town, the occasion, he announced, being an anniversary of the Battle of Balaclava. A dozen or so officers were present, resplendent, as he was himself, in the braided and colourful uniform of the cavalry officer. There were also attending cavalry bandsmen to give musical entertainment.

After a sumptuous meal, with much liquor, the officers were shown round The Alma residence. In many of the apartments, along with military mementos, such as sabres and other hand weapons, some of them primitive, there were other tokens of the family's service to the British Empire, including portraits of the Brigadier's parent, Sir Bertran Caden-Cole and other deceased relatives. The Brigadier escorted his guests to the top storey of the residence. There they were brought to a large apartment known as the nursery.

It was a veritable museum of children's toys or play-things. There were wooden and cardboard models of castles and fortresses. Indeed, the military character of the museum was emphasised by the phalanxes of model lead soldiers ranged on shelves in the apartment. These were mostly of the mounted kind, their mounts ranging from horses and mules to camels and elephants, all richly caparisoned. They were accompanied by model artillery and wagons with stores.

It was here, apparently, the Brigadier had spent much of his childhood, as he took pride in explaining to his guests, detailing how some of his ancestors had associations with some of the regiments modelled on the shelves. The toy he finally dilated about was a large rocking horse. It was the size of a small pony and still harnessed with bridle, reins, saddle and stirrups, its hooves firm on the rockers, it was still mobile.

The interest of a group of the officers seemed centred on the rocking-horse as the Brigadier, handling the reins, demonstrated the mount's easy back-and-forward movement. Suddenly he braced himself and mounted on to the saddle. With his chest flaunted, the light from the ceiling glinting, on the seried medals on his left breast and, above, on the regimental insignia fronting his plumed hat, he commanded one of the officers to hand him a sabre from weapons clustered on one of the nursery walls. Armed with this, he kept thrusting it to left and right, the while he kept declaiming lines from Tennyson's *Charge of the Light Brigade*. With the rocking thus accelerated the mount's rockers kept shifting to claim more floor space in the nursery, the officers, now forming a circle tending to move back. Suddenly the Brigadier seemed stricken with some kind of seizure, in moments collapsing from the saddle and falling to the floor. When some of the officers hurried to attempt succour it was found that the Brigadier when falling on the floor had impaled part of his body on the sabre.

Whether it was loss of blood from this, or heart attack, or stroke caused the quick-ensuing death was not, it appears, established. What was established was that when The Templars heard of the incident, it was to remain long the subject of their discussions. They thought it made a memorable tale, how the doughty Brigadier had attained glory in Britain's wars abroad, to come home to meet an inglorious end riding his rocking horse.

I suppose it was appropriate that this reminiscing and phantasising in my notebook should end at this point on a military note or scene. I was now returned from the Wimireux Cookery School to the infantry base depot at Étaples, where I was assigned as officers' cook to the Second-Fifth Battalion of the King's Own Royal Lancaster Regiment. I, of course, had no say in the assignment. At the depot arrivals were assigned or posted to units as reinforcements were needed in the different units at the front.

The King's Own Royal Lancasters were a unit in the Fifty-fifth Division, which was then on active service in the war zone in front of Arras, then occupied by the Germans. Travelling by lorry I was delivered at the headquarters of the battalion, which was then at rest in a village behind the fighting lines. Normally there were three lines, the front line, the support line and the reserve line, with communicating trenches between the lines. The distance between the lines might be a quarter of a mile, perhaps more, perhaps less.

It was now February, 1918; and through the Winter on this part of the war front there had been little fighting, and as a result the army sappers had had opportunity to build strong defensive positions in the way of well-constructed trenches and dugouts. The general routine was the battalion, relieving another battalion in the division, would do about a fortnight's service in the fighting lines, withdrawing to rest camp when relieved by some other divisional unit.

The rest camp might be eight or ten kilometres behind the reserve line. The camp's situation would usually be near a village or perhaps more populated centre where there were stores and estaminets or cafes, permitting such social distraction for the soldiers as unfamiliarity with the French language would permit. Often accommodation in the rest camps would be under canvas; and here the danger from bombardment by long-range artillery from the front or from enemy aeroplanes making night raids was often greater than might be experienced in the better defended trenches at the front.

A feature of this rest camp on the Arras front was the boxing ring at its centre. I saw the posts of the ring used for the tying-up of soldiers who for breaches of military discipline had been sentenced to so many hours or days to field punishment number 1. In a wooded area the punishment might be administered by tying the culprit to a tree. I understand in artillery units the delinquents were tied to gun-wheels.

The tying-up chastisement was known as the crucifixion punishment; and, apparently, the idea behind it was that the culprit being thus publicly pilloried would incite the opprobrium or scorn of his colleagues. It did not seem to have had that effect. If anything the sight of a captive strung-up to a ring post had more the effect of evoking sympathy in his colleagues. Perhaps it was the natural response of those already chafing under the constraints normal to military life.

This punishment was prescribed in the case of comparatively mild breaches of discipline when the offences were committed on active service in the line, as the actual fighting area was called. Such breaches might be minor insubordination, assaults on superiors, wilful destruction of military property, thefts from colleagues. Such misdemeanours could thus be dealt with in the area or sector of active service. Only the more serious military offences, such as gross insubordination, incitement to mutiny, desertion from the fighting area would be likely to eventuate in removal from the area to face court-martial and possible sentence to be shot by firing squad.

The sight of the boxing ring in the rest camp evoked memories of experiences in that sport in earlier days. I remembered I was still going to school in Dundalk when a few of us, pupils in the Irish Christian Brothers' school, started a boxing club in an apartment of an unoccupied house in a laneway some of us had to pass along on our way from Clanbrassil Street to the school. A few years later, when domiciled in Dublin and working at night in Johnston, Mooney & O'Brien's bakery in Ballsbridge, I was associated with a few of the younger workers in starting a boxing club in a mews or rear apartment of a house in Beechwood Avenue, Ranelagh, a suburb of the city. Though in both these cases boxing was the main activity engaged in, other sports, including wrestling and weight-lighting and general physical culture also attracted us.

Indeed, I was to find that my interest in what was then called the Noble Art was more in the negative side of mastering feints and stratagems that would outwit the opponent rather than the placing of blows that would punish him into submission.

I had still this attitude to the sport when I first saw the boxing ring in that rest camp in the Arras sector of the front. Yet I volunteered to enter a boxing competition which was being organised there as part of the distractions or recreation to engage the soldiers in their brief interval from the fighting line. What were my reasons for this, entering the lightweight, 9 stone 7 pounds, class of the competitions? There was the reason that the spell of training which entrance in the competitions would require would be a welcome relief from involvement in the routine of drills and fatigues which life in the camp normally entailed. But there was the more important reason of giving boost to my morale. I wanted to establish that though a conscientious objector to doing military service in the British Army, I was not a pacifist but ready to assert myself in self-defence or, indeed, in a cause in which I believed.

This brought me to considering how far my history of conscientious objection was known to those I now had to consort with in this stage of my experiences. I was certain these ordinary colleagues I now found myself among in the regiment knew nothing of my army history. They regarded me as the ordinary infantryman the circumstances of the war had brought them into contact with. They might have seen me as having exceptional traits in being interested in the French language and in literary and political topics in which they had little or no interest. Yet some of the officers of the regiment, certainly the commanding officer, the adjutant and the head of the redcaps or military police would be acquainted with my record. As to lower ranks in the regiment I had a suspicion that Lance corporal Hobbes, my immediate non-commissioned officer in my cooking duties, had some knowledge of my history. He was an Australian who was still mourning for the loss of a brother killed in service with the Australian army. Known to be Irish, I could hardly have escaped being called Paddy in the regiment, and, indeed, in contacts in the army generally. In my company the Lance corporal was fond of berating the Paddies, citing how the Easter Week Republicans tried to stab Britain in the back.

I had, I think, three turns of this rotating between the front or firing lines and the rest camp. For most of the time there was little action beyond the routine daily shelling against which, save in a few instances, the well-constructed trenches and dugouts were effective defences. Sometimes we had to do reconnoitring patrols above the trenches and into no-man's land, the area before the enemy's trenches. These patrols were usually made up from a call for volunteers. But the call was often made with the officer, usually a sergeant calling: 'I want four volunteers, you, you, you and you', the call indicating the individuals wanted.

I was once on a daylight patrol in an area between the front line and the support line. It was to rescue some men thought to have been wounded by shellfire. We came across a number of men braced against a bank of earth, their features set like statues, grey and wildly staring, but seemingly with no abrasion or bruise on them. They had been killed by a shell explosion. They had no marks of blood. Blood was to be seen nearby, on clumps of primroses. These had come as augurs of Spring. What else did they augur? Later I was to attempt a poem on this feature of the incident.

Another patrol experience was at night in no-man's land. The purpose of this exercise was to probe the advanced posts of the enemy. It was a patrol all but the reckless or foolhardy wanted to avoid. We had come to a point in the area that was being exposed by cascading verey-lights shot into no-man's land from the enemy's observation posts. One of the verey-lights dropped near me and set alight some inflammable material. I saw a petrol tin standing near-by, and, as such was being used for the transport of water to the trenches, I assumed it contained water and threw it on to the burning material. There was an immediate burst of flame that lit much of the area around. It soon revealed our position and a concentration of enemy fire from machine guns and trench-mortars was directed on us.

All of us were lucky to have found our way safely back from the patrol. When investigated Lance corporal Hobbes wanted to make a big point of the fact that I, if unwittingly, was responsible for the blaze in no-man's land that drew the enemy fire. But his senior, Corporal Price, who was also on the patrol went out of his way to stress the accidental nature of the occurrence. Corporal Price was one of few I met in the British Army with whom I was to have a brief friendship. He had education and tastes somewhat above the standards one encountered in the British Army at that time.

The problems of cooking in the trenches were a daily worry, particularly in catering for the officers where the standards contrived to be higher than for the rank-and-file. For the rank-and-file the food was conveyed by the commissariat in rations mostly of preserved foods of tinned pork-and-beans, corned beef, mobile boilers of meat or mutton stew and soup, potatoes and other kinds of vegetables. There were the boilers containing tea. These comestibles were ladled into the soldier's mess-tin, part of the equipment he carried on his person.

For the officers the catering was more sophisticated. An effort had to be made to supplement or substitute these prepared rations with fresh foods in meats and other comestibles that might be commissioned or requisitioned from local traders behind the line. Whilst soldiers of the rank-and-file would contrive to have their meals al fresco, in the open trenches, sometimes on the fire-step, the officers would be catered for in the dugouts. These earth-works, sometimes thirty to forty feet underground were often elaborate structures. They would have cooking facilities and stores, mess, sleeping and toilet facilities for the officers, their servants and the cooking staff. The servants acted as waiters to the officers at meals in the mess.

The rank-and-file, of course, had their dugouts, at similar depths as the officers, but not as elaborately appointed. Sleeping in the dug-outs meant bedding down in one's clothes, perhaps at times with one's equipment on, and never without one's rifle or other arms.

In the rest camp we found irksome the sometimes resorted to discipline of the barrack square, the seemingly pointless drills and fatigues. But up the line, as duty in the trenches was called, these irksome exercises were replaced by the discipline of danger, a drill-master uttering commands more potent than any that could be barked by barrack-square marionette, commands made with the seldom resting insistence of rifle and machine-gun fire, and emphasised by the plonks of trench mortars and shells. In the trenches the rituals of button-polishing and spring-to-attention tended to dissolve into something approaching a camaraderie between the rank-and-file and the officers. One was reminded of the story in the battalion of an officer who through over officiousness in the trenches was made a casualty not by enemy fire but at the hands of some one or ones under his command.

We entered and, when our spell was over, vacated the trenches by way of the third or reserve line. This abutted on to a sunken road which was itself an enlarged trench permitting of something like normal traffic for the provision of supplies. When, replaced by the relieving unit, we emerged from the trenches and were mustered on the sunken road, we would see assembled there the battalion brass and reed band and a bevy of well-groomed horses with their attendants. The concourse would be quickly marshalled, the officers taking to their mounts and heading their respective companies, the battalion officer and his staff in front, behind the band. The band would strike up popular rather than martial airs.

At this stage the trench mood of something like tolerance between rank-and-file and officers would be still surviving. I have a memory of one of the mounted officers being made fun of on the march to the rest camp. One of the company commanders, Captain Bennett, one of the least popular officers with the rank-and-file, usually made awkward mount and posture on his horse. From some of the ranks behind him on the march campwards this evoked a chant to the rhythm of the drum-beat 'Now he's up Now he's down'

As we approached the rest camp such levity subsided and thoughts centred more on speculating on whatever might be the camp authorities plans for diversion or entertainment during our all too brief sojourn there. Recitals by the battalion band would figure much in the programmes. Though the band's signature tune was an excerpt from Donezetti 's *Daughter of the Regiment*, it rarely discoursed operatic pieces, its repertoire was usually made up of musical comedy excerpts and other numbers popular at the time. Sometimes there was entertainment of the music-hall variety kind, when there would be brief visits by concert-party professionals from Britain. Such diversions, with sports competitions, would soften a bit the relapse to drilling and other boring routines which seem an inescapable accompaniment to military life. An initial introduction to these, of course, were the medical inspections and delousing operations immediately following arrival at the camp.

A few weeks service in the trenches without even once divesting oneself of one's clothes bred lice, and this, as well as adding to the hardship of trench life, tended to foster the transmission of disease. In the trenches, after long spells of duties, it was not unusual for men, distracted with lice on their bodies, to have recourse to burying their shirts and underclothes in the earth for a period to exterminate the vermin. In the rest camp this was achieved by depositing the clothes, and sometimes the uniforms, in the fumigating chambers, an essential part of the rest camp equipment.

I had three turns of these alternating visits or spells in the line or trenches and the rest camp, and for the most part I had seen very little actual fighting, or the results of such, in sights of dead or badly mutilated combatants. Of course, the sector in which I was happened to be a quiet one. Life in a war sector tends to breed a kind of isolation or provincialism. Secrecy pervades; one will not know what is going on in a neighbouring sector, much less what is happening in the war as a whole.

Though this quiet went on in the sector for a few weeks there were rumours daily of impending action. There were signs evident that the Germans were well advanced in preparations for a spring offensive. Confirmation of this had been forthcoming from prisoners captured in raids of the German lines and from scans of the enemy's lines and communications made by the observations balloons high above the British positions. It was during my third spell in the trenches that the German's offensive started. That was on the twenty-first of March, 1918. It was heralded at dawn by a massive bombardment of the British lines. The bombardment was of the concentrated kind known as drum-fire, the persistent whizzing and exploding of shells resembling in rhythm frequency, but scarcely in the horrendousness of sound, the tapping of a rallentando on a drum.

The technique of the massed artillery barrage was to concentrate the fire first on the front-line positions. Then when it is judged that all in the front-line have been put out of action, the barrage is lifted to involve the second or support line. This is to hinder reinforcements in that line advancing through the communicating trenches to attempt to hold or recover positions in the front line. That accomplished, the barrage shifts to fall on the third or reserve line, with the same intention of preventing reinforcement of any of the front position.

When the offensive started that morning I was in the reserve or third line. We were in one of the dugouts of the battalion headquarters. The order was given: Stand to! There was a hurried scamper from the bunks, and with adjustments of equipment and arms we were marshalled to proceed through the communication trench to the support line. The communication trenches were now being involved in the bombardment and there were casualties among us from shrapnel wounds. These were left behind to await being tended to by the Red Cross Corps.

We succeeded in getting to the support or second line, where the barrage was now being concentrated, a fact attested by the number of casualties already accounted for there. Ordered further along the communicating trenches we eventually, with continuing losses from shellfire, found ourselves in the front-line. Here there were even more casualties. An intermission from the bombardment, now concentrated on the second and third lines, had permitted of first-aid being given the wounded. Some were already dead, and help was being concentrated on the more seriously wounded cases, that were making known their sufferings in groans and calls for help.

Some of us, now regarded as reinforcements, were ordered onto the fire-steps of the trenches, in replacement of those fallen. The fire-step of the trench is the raised part of it that fronts no-man's-land and enables one to survey that area and direct weapon-fire at the enemy positions. I was not long on the fire-step when the non-commissioned officer in charge of the platoon drew my attention to the fact that the rising sun was making a glare on the bayonet pointing upwards from the rifle at my side. The glare might be seen in no-man's-land and beyond, and might thereby be a target for the enemy. No sooner had I taken steps to deal with this danger than there was a whizz and explosion in the air just above our part of the trench.

It seems it was a small shell or trench mortar. A large fragment of it hit the platoon non-commissioned officer on the head, mortally wounding him. I was lucky to escape with shrapnel wound in my left arm and thumb. I tried to stop rather profuse bleeding with the first-aid kit, which all soldiers on active service in the war theatres then carried in a small pocket attached to their jacket. When more serious cases were attended to, and, with several dead, removed by the first-aid unit, I was permitted by the new platoon commander to leave the trench and follow the others through the communication trenches en route to the casualty clearing station at some distance along the sunken road where the reserve line abutted.

It took a long time, and more casualties were suffered, in making progress through the communication trenches. The bombardment was now being joined by the enemy aircraft, and the action was being concentrated on the rear of the front to hinder the arrival of reinforcements and supplies. When we succeeded in making our way through the shell-holes and debris of the communication trenches, and gaining exit onto the sunken road, our further progress towards the casualty clearing station was halted by a squad of red-caps. They interrogated all the wounded to satisfy themselves that they were genuine casualties. The red caps had short arms in their hands. I learned afterwards that where they found any of the ranks leaving the trenches unwounded or unauthorised, they deemed them deserters, and on the refusal of such to return to the trenches they were summarily shot on the spot.

We were conveyed in ambulances and lorries from the sunken road along a few miles to the casualty clearing station. This was a field hospital situated at Doulens, a small French town. Much of the hospital was under canvas. I was among the less serious cases, and, as stretchers and ambulances were arriving with more seriously wounded, in some cases badly mutilated casualties, we had to wait for attention. Medical attention was being concentrated on summary blood transfusions and amputations. The cries and lamentations and often curses in the field hospital were a depressing obligato to the still audible barrage over the war front.

When I was injected against tetanus and had my wounds dressed I was directed to join an ambulance train preparatory to what was to be a long journey to Boulogne. We had delays where the line had been bombed by enemy planes. Arrived at Boulogne, some of us were transferred to lorries in which we made almost as tedious journey South to the rural district of Bushy. There we were received into another field hospital or, perhaps more correctly, convalescent camp. Here the patients were mostly walking cases, some of them not suffering from wounds, but recovering from fevers or other maladies as a result of service in war zone. The place was in a beautiful setting of sylvan and hilly surrounds, obtruding sounds come only from the swirl or eddies of brooks and the calls of birds. It was such a pleasant contrast to the death dealing pandemonium of the war front.

The Bushy field hospital or convalescent home had contrived programmes of distractions or recreation more varied and interesting than was the case in the rest camp, and there were no drills or fatigues. Yet for many of the patients in the place there must have been the abiding anxiety of impending end of the sojourn and probable return to the combat zone. It was common knowledge in the place that there were patients deliberately thwarting recovery to prolong their stay and dodge being declared fit and ready for active service again. Some were resorting to self-infliction of disabilities to delay their exit. A common form of this was to chew and ingest the cordite in a bullet cartridge. This had the effect of sending up the temperature and making the person feverish. A similar effect was to be had by impregnating a cigarette with drops of iodine and inhaling the smoke.

Though I contemplated my impending discharge from the place and my probable return to the fighting zone, with much anxiety, I could not but regard such self-infliction as a contemptible form of poltroonery.

I was to be six weeks in the Bushy convalescent camp, my treatment there being concerned not just with my not very serious wounds, but with my debilitated state of health, brought on by my experiences in the war zone. Much that preoccupied my thoughts in Bushy centred on my probable early return to the war front. In respite from this I again had recourse to notebook and pencil. I again fell to reminiscence and fancy, conjuring scene and incident, sometimes inventing them.

*Alice Deane (1861-1918),
Dundalk, c. 1890, mother
of John Swift.*

*Patrick Swift (1858-1926),
Dundalk, c.1890,
father of John Swift.*

Clanbrassil Street, Dundalk, c. 1900.

The building on the left-hand side towards the end of the street, number 83, with the large exposed gable bearing the almost indecipherable names of Swift and Cooper, was the birthplace of John Swift and the premises of his family's bakery business. A few doors beyond on the left, number 77, was the home of the Swifts from c. 1899 to c. 1909. The tavern in the last building on the right-hand side of the street, with the large exposed gable, number 15, was the haunt of Patrick Swift and his coterie.

[Photo: Courtesy of the National Library of Ireland]

John (Johnny) Swift and Frances Swift,
uncle and aunt of John Swift c.1890

'Dundalk Democrat' advertisement
announcing the opening of Swift, Reilly & Co's
bread and confectionery bakeries and shop on
13 February 1891.
[Photo: Courtesy of Dundalk Public Library]

Fergus White, cousin of John Swift, at Toberona (John's Well),
Dundalk, 4 October 2006.

*83 Clanbrassil Street, Dundalk, c. 1986, birthplace of John Swift on
26 August 1896, and premises of his family's bakeries and shop.*
[Photo: Don McLave]

77 Clanbrassil Street, Dundalk, c. 1986,
home of the Swifts from c.1899 to c.1909.
[Photo: Don McLave]

*15 Clanbrassil Street, Dundalk, c.1986, formerly Conlon's
(actually Connolly's) tavern, haunt of Patrick Swift and his coterie.*
[Photo: Don McLave]

Dr. Michael C. Moynagh (died 1912),
Crown Solicitor for Co. Louth,
first employer of John Swift.

Dr. Edmund F. Flood
(died 1922),
a musical guest of the Swift family.

Tom V. Parkes (1854-1913),
the most celebrated musician of his
era in Dundalk.

Michael Deane (c. 1840-1928),
great-uncle of John Swift.

Mary (May) Bridget Swift (1903-1953) and
Patrick (Paddy) James Swift (1904-1960),
sister and brother of John Swift,
Dublin, c. 1916.

John Swift, aged 22, following the
Armistice for World War 1, in Germany,
in late 1918 or early 1919.

John Swift, aged 22, with the Second Fifth Battalion, (55th Division),
of the King's Own Royal Lancasters, following the Armistice for
World War 1, in Germany, in late 1918 or early 1919.

From left:
Harry White (1898-1970),
first cousin of John Swift,
and John Swift aged
approximately 27, c. 1924.
[Photo: Julia Farrell]

John Swift,
aged approximately 29,
Dublin, c. 1925.

The Bakery Trade's Social Club Committee 1927-1934.
Standing, from left: Paddy Swift, Billy Kinsella, Michael Walsh, J. Swan, T. McElroy;
Sitting, from left: Tommy McQuillan (Secretary), Paddy Hogan (Trustee),
John Swift (President), Paddy McDarby (Treasurer) and Dick Sheeran (Trustee)

From left: John Swift and Seán Lemass, Minister for Industry and Commerce,
admiring the exhibits at the International Bakery Exhibition,
in the Mansion House, Dublin, on 3 August 1953.

Four Provinces House mural 1946, by Frances Kelly, depicting the Lord Mayor fulfilling his duty to check the weight of bread in the market, bread being sold by weight in earlier times

Four Provinces House mural 1946, by Nano Reid, depicting procession of the Dublin trades' guilds, with the Bakers' banner on the right

*Four Provinces House mural 1946, by Nano Reid, depicting the
co-operative experiment at Ralahine, Co. Clare, 1831-1833*

*Four Provinces House mural 1946, by Nano Reid, depicting
James Connolly organising the Belfast Branch of the ITGWU in 1911.*

*John Swift speaking at a social function in the Four Provinces House Library
in the late 1940s.*

Four Provinces House
Library

G. Bernard Shaw

Ayot Saint Lawrence

9th October 1947

 FOUR PROVINCES HOUSE
HARCOURT STREET
DUBLIN

1937.

*Four Provinces House Library - form of volume of
'The Complete Plays of Bernard Shaw', signed by the author, 9 October 1947.*

John Swift,
aged approximately 58, c.1954.

John Swift, aged 60,
Dublin, 27 April 1957.

The Swift family, from left: (Patrick) Grosvenor, Harriet, John, Alice and John,
Dublin, 16 July 1960.

Harriet Swift (née Hendy) (1911-1990) and John Swift, aged 71,
Dublin, August 1966.

John Swift, aged approximately 68, and Harriet Swift, guests at a trade union convention in the USA, mid-1960s.

John Swift, aged 77, at the Inaugural General Meeting of the Irish Labour History Society, Newman House, St. Stephen's Green, Dublin, on 27 October 1973.

Flanked by, from left, Ruairi Quinn, TD, Deputy Leader, and Dick Spring, TD, Leader of the Labour Party, John Swift, aged 93, at a Labour Party social function in his honour, in Dáil Éireann, Dublin, on 6 December 1989.

Chapter 7

I don't know what might be the incidence of females of our species being born without hair or prospects of hair on their heads. I believe it is quite rare in the male. And I am sure the incidence of such will be likely to bring much chagrin to the person born to bear the deprivation. He will be fated to go through life with the description bald, or, indeed, with the contemptuous form of the term, baldy. In an age that has all but abandoned wigs, he will be likely to have recourse to one or other of the different forms of head-dress resorted to by males, the choice usually to be determined by the current fashion in hats or caps, and in some cases to be influenced by the professional or social status of the person concerned. Who will know how often the royal crown or the priest's mitre has been the welcome refuge of the bald, a welcome resource to compensate deprivation?

Whilst studies of the male in recent decades may disclose he is not disposed as he was to head-cover, research into earlier decades will likely show as strong a reluctance of the male to going bareheaded as would be to leaving naked for public exhibition that similarly spheroid or curvaceous part of his anatomy, his posterior.

Mention of such brings to mind an incident, or story of an incident told me many years later by my much revered but now deceased friend, Robert Hannan. Robert had become a student in Dublin's Trinity College, entered there with his parents' wish that he would take to studies in Trinity's School of Divinity, to become a reverend of the Church of Ireland. Robert had other ideas, going on to make philosophy his main study, eventually taking his moderatorship under Professor Macran, then prominent as a Kantian and Hegelian scholar.

At the time the Rev. Dr. Luce was head of the School of Divinity. He was a tall, thin, acetic-looking man, completely without hair on his head. It was said he had never tried to hide this lack of coiffure on his cranium, being, it seems, reluctant to wear even that head-dress or diadem of the professional scholar, the mortar-board.

Dr. Luce was bathing on the strand of the Dublin north suburb, Dollymount. He was in a shallow part of the tide, hunkered in a stretched position, his head bobbing up and down in the water. An elderly lady of the Dublin Molly Malone street-trader type, seated not far distant on the strand, had been watching the mild acrobatics, specially noting the bobbing cranium. Shocked at the sight, she shouted at him 'Go down, y'owl divil, and come up daycent'.

Algernon Cecil Darleigh had been born without hair on his head or any sign thereon of the likelihood of a coiffeured future. Had medical science at the time had any resources to remedy the lack, Algernon's parents would have quickly availed of them. The family was well off, with a considerable estate in North County Louth, near Ardee. The family was prominent in county society, mixing as they did with their near neighbours, the Bellinghams, then, at the Northern end of the County, with such as the Caden-Coles and the Clifford-Muirs. They followed the Louth fox-hunt and were equally keen followers of the Marquis of Conyngham's otter-hunting pack. Professionally, most of the males of the Darleigh family had over generations followed careers in the British civil and military services, some of them rising to position of governorship in the British colonies.

Young Algernon had got this, his first Christian name from his uncle, his father's younger brother. Shortly after the christening the uncle had fallen into bad company, scamps much inferior to him in class, among whom he became known as Algy. This had much distressed the family, not least young Algernon himself. Uncle Algernon had been reported in drunken brawls resulting in assaults on people and damage to property. In consequence of these, and other misdemeanours involving young women, he had accumulated debts, all of much embarrassment to the family.

When reports of these happenings were circulating preparations were being made to send young Algernon to one of the superior public schools in England. Up to this the boy's education had been taken care of by private tutors. With this new turn in his upbringing, this going out into a new and larger world, young Algernon had certain apprehensions, not the least of them fear of his name, as in the case of his uncle's, becoming truncated, or done violence to. The fear became a phobia with him. Public schools were notorious for the mutilation and vulgarising of proper names and coining of nicknames. He resolved he would keep away as much as possible from getting involved in groups or gangs in the school. He would keep himself out of their games and pranks.

Now entered, he was slow to make friends or chums among the other pupils. Watching them in the quadrangle rushing out to the sports pitches, had one of them dared to address him as Algy he would have felt it as the amputation of a limb, and, unconsciously perhaps would have limped and hobbled. But, it turned out, he had his fears for nothing. Algernon was to go through all his terms in the school holding his name intact. Perhaps it was his timorousness or diffidence had bred in his school mates that indulgence or pity we sometimes show the deprived. When they, tutors as well as fellow pupils, addressed him as Algernon, as they always did, perhaps it was in the consciousness that his lack of hair was sufficient loss to bear without depriving his name of a syllable and vulgarising it.

Finishing school, he had now to consider what career he would embark on. Here he hesitated, in the same trepidation as when he entered the Public School. He was still being pursued by the phobias about his name and his bald pate when he thought of entering medical school to become a doctor. But he reflected on the medical students he had known and how they were as ready as any in taking liberties with names, as industrious as any in coining nicknames. Examining the possibilities in other professions, including the higher civil service, Algernon came to the conclusion that the law would be the one profession in which respect for the proper dignity of things, including nomenclature, would be likely to be honoured.

In making this his choice of profession Algernon was concerned not only with maintaining the dignity of his name but also with the consideration that should he attain to the higher ranks of the law, say, to becoming barrister, senior counsel or judge, he would also attain to the professional right of wearing a wig. Thoughts of becoming a judge became dazzling to the youth. Here, indeed, one soared above the usage of mere Christian names, however prestigious. Once a judge, one would be addressed as Your Worship, Your Lordship'. Even the newspapers would accord him Mr Justice Darleigh

Algernon's parents had left the choice of his career largely to himself; and in due course he entered the Dublin Law School, to study for the Bar. He was diligent at his studies and soon qualified as a barrister. He started his work as advocate when Davitt's land agitation and the sporadic actions of the Fenians' successors were involving the courts in much work. Darleigh's work, by his own preference, went more in civil cases, property inheritance and business contract litigation, slander and libel actions. Sooner than was usual with junior advocates, he became a senior counsel, and, not long after that, a judge of the circuit court, taking cases at quarter sessions.

I still remember how in Dundalk the opening of these sessions was the occasion of great pomp and ceremony. Many of the townsfolk would turn out to watch the progress of the sessions judges in their cavalcade from their private lodgings in Barrack Street to the Market Square in front of the Courthouse. Arrayed in their robes and wigs, they would come in their carriage drawn by opulent-looking horses, and escorted by a troop of huzzars or lancers, their mounts as lordly-looking and their sabres or lances glinting light. As the posse lined up in the Square the judges would dismount and, led by the tipstaff, they would enter the Courthouse with great solemnity.

Judge Darleigh was to spend a decade or so on the quarter sessions circuit. The time was at the end of the nineteenth century's last decade, the beginning of which had seen the political fall and demise of Parnell. There was still much disorder in the country, with resistance to evictions and suppression of meetings. As the new century dawned the national spirit was expressing itself in art, in what was called the Celtic revival.

The Abbey Theatre Company from Dublin was visiting Dundalk, and crowds were filling the Town Hall for dramatic presentations by Yeats, Lady Gregory and Synge. There was a revival of interest in the Irish language, an interest that extended to other aspects of the native culture. The resurgence of nationalism had concentrated the interest on the old Celtic legends, the sagas about the Fianna. Local bodies like the County Louth Archeological Society had encouraged this revival of national interest, and, I believe, the Society was associated with promoting the pageants some of which I saw at the Cuchulainn Fort out at Castletown, a mile or so from Dundalk town. The pageants, perhaps extravagantly dressed in the costumes thought appropriate to the times being portrayed, drew large crowds of spectators from the town. They came to see presented the fabled chiefs and warriors of the Fianna, Cuchulainn, Finn MacCool, Uisinn, Oscar. Some of the women of the legends were also portrayed including Emer, Saba, Deirdre, Maeve. These ladies were gowned in such elegance that one wondered how they could have got about in what would appear to have been the never ending battling and jousting of the Fianna.

It would appear that Judge Darleigh before he retired had become a member of the Louth Archaeological Society. One of the cases or series of cases he had had to deal with in the quarter sessions court in the town was a political disturbance that occurred at one of the Fianna pageants. It was fomented by some republican, anti-British sympathisers in the crowd. When the police intervened it was not clear how two of the performers in the pageant became involved, to be later charged by the police.

The two were named Philip Crowe, the hairdresser encountered in The Temple tavern, and a young woman reputed a local beauty, Gráinne Daragh. He was performing in the tableau as Finn MacCool, and she taking the part of MacCool's wife, Saba. Though the police made strong cases against all the accused, these two main performers were dealt lightly with by Judge Darleigh. He bound them over to keep the peace. Perhaps he was influenced in this by the appearance and bearing of the two participants. The young man portraying Finn was of fine physique, and well-cut features, crowned with a mass of auburn hair tending to curls. She, with darker tresses, was equally well featured and developed and was of much the same age as her consort, around the mid-twenties.

It was shortly after this Judge Darleigh decided to retire from the bench. He was now finding himself more and more out of sympathy acting for the crown, and more taken up or interested in local cultural activities. Besides, he was still suffering from the effects, a noticeable limp, from a hunting accident which befell him some years earlier. When he retired he decided to reside in the select boarding-house where the judges put-up in their quarter sessions visits to Dundalk.

In his retirement Algernon Cecil Darleigh, though still saluted as Judge, gradually got away from his more sedentary pursuits. He was now frequently seen at the local performances of the Abbey Players and other dramatic and concert groups visiting the town. He had taken to reading authors such as Shaw and Wilde. More, whilst a strict teetotaller during his bench and earlier days, he was now clinking glasses with local ex-colleagues of his profession, and disposed to extend further social contacts. Among those with whom he had sought to become more acquainted were the pair he first met when they came before his bench following the pageant fracas in Castletown now some years before, Phil Crowe and his MacCool consort Saba, Gráinne Daragh. She had since married, but shortly after the marriage was made a widow.

Philip Crowe, as well as running the flourishing hairdressing business in Earl Street, had many private clients in the town whom he visited in their homes in the course of his trade. Among them were several prominent in public life and in the professions. These preferred private service to having to sit and wait in the public saloon, there to have to listen to the chatter and banter of the common clientele come in from the street. The retired judge was one of Crowe's private clients. The hairdresser came to his boarding house almost daily, to attend to the judge's shave, an operation which when performed by himself the judge had found more and more disagreeable owing to the increasing discomfort suffered in the accident.

Another service proffered by the hairdresser in these visits was the advice and later the work tendered the judge in the matter of wigs. Though retired from the law Judge Darleigh had not dispensed with wigs. True, he had laid aside his judge's wig; but he had procured himself a simpler coiffeur, one more on the lines of the barrister's wig. This had been supplied him by well-known firm of wig-makers in London. The judge, still most sensitive about his baldness, never appeared, whether in the boarding house or out somewhere in the town, without wearing his head-piece.

How often has crown or mitre been worn and held with tenaciousness, not just as symbolising power or prestige, but that it hid a bald head?

Though differing so much in education and social backgrounds, there were certain common factors attracting the hairdresser and the judge to one another. There was the matter of his phobias, the judge still went in dread of the truncation of his primary Christian name, whilst the hairdresser was still a refugee from a nickname. It will be remembered how Phil Crowe was driven from the select lounge or snug of a tavern by the ruling habitués there conferring on him the nickname Curley. In attempted refuge from that he had taken himself to an inferior snug, and, more, had made vain attempt to rid himself of the curls. The judge's preoccupation with wigs prompted the hairdresser's increased interest in the subject. He already had some experience in the making of wigs, and in their maintenance and repair. He had some knowledge of the materials and shaping of the different classes of wigs in the legal profession, the half-hearted one of counsel that but partly covered the head and tapered at the back into a fringe of scuts and tails, and the more ample locks of the judge that cascaded in flounces on to the shoulders, in token, apparently, of the weight of perspicacity and responsibility to be borne by the wearer.

Though the judge and the hairdresser had a common concern for the integrity of names their attitudes differed in the respect that whilst the former dreaded the abbreviation of his name Algernon to the vulgar Algy, the latter had welcomed the shortening of his name from Philip to Phil. Was not Phil the root or gravamen of those words of lovely, nay, noble connotations, philosophy and philanthropy, the former denoting love of learning and wisdom, the latter, love of being kind and charitable

Phil Crowe had become well known in the town, if only for his peregrinations in service to his clients domiciled in the town's better areas. Always well-dressed, in dark clothes with frock coat, and with felt-hat tall enough to serve as treasure chest to the copious coiffure, shielding its coils and quiffs from the vagaries of the weather. In the streets, though pleasant-looking and affable, he walked portentously, one hand fingering a bemedaled gold watch-chain stretching from one pocket of his waistcoat to the other, his other hand engaged in carrying a large brown-leather portmanteau. A smaller convenience would have sufficed to carry the normal requisites of the hairdresser, the scissors and hairbrush, the razor, soap and soap-brush, the pomade and lotion.

But hairdresser Crowe's needs and interests extended further, so that his portmanteau contained as well various bottles of chemical liquids and cases of powder. These were properties which he kept away from the shelves of his saloon and even from safe recesses in his home. They were the materials he was using in his researches. With them he hoped to compound a substance that he would patent as an effective hair-restorer or rather hair creator, for there were those bald that never had hair. Here, of course, Judge Darleigh was keenly interested, and ever ready to hear what progress, if any, the hairdresser had to report.

It was probable the judge had his doubts about the hoped-for success of Crowe's researches. The judge had learned of how the hairdresser was known to be very credulous and inclined to phantasise. For instance in the hearing of some acquaintances he had claimed that Crowe Street, near which he had his business, had been called after a celebrity forbear of his. He claimed further that the town's arms, the shield bearing three crows, had been copied from his family's escutcheon of hundreds of years ago. Crowe's credulousness had scarcely lessened with his experiences in performing in the Fianna pageants in Castletown. The seriousness with which these old legends were now being taken in what was to become known as the Celtic revival had no doubt had its effects on some of the youth of Crowe's generation. People like Crowe would have come to regard Cuchulainn as a Dundalk man of his time, as real as, say, the current Chairman of the town's Urban Council.

The judge's misgivings about Phil Crowe's researches were strengthened when the hairdresser announced to him that he was going to do some experiments in the lake near the top of Slieve Gullion. This was part of the range of mountains in South Armagh that ran close to the border with County Louth. Slieve Gullion figured in an episode narrated of Finn MacCool, the Fianna hero portrayed by Phil Crowe in the Fianna pageants. Finn had come to the Gullion Lake to bathe in its waters. He was reputed to be an expert swimmer. He was resting on the bank when a woman came into sight. She had once been a suitor for Finn's favours, and now, her once felt jealousy of the rival, Saba, Finn had married, had turned to hatred of him. Unseen by him, she took a jewel from her gown and cast it in the lake. She then pleaded to Finn to recover it. Finn dived into the lake and recovered the jewel from the bottom. When he swam to the surface again he was seen to have become bald, with his face and body wrinkled and old-looking.

This was narrated as happening on the South side of the lake. It was said also that on the North side the water there if contacted in the upsurge of a certain spring eddying up from the bottom had qualities that would make hair grow and flourish. The account went that the spring here came from a source under the lake that sent a current in the direction of the opposite or Southern side of the lake. The current coursed through a channel of earth and rock impregnated with poisonous matter, contaminating the water on its way to spurt a spring from the lake bottom on the Southern side.

It was here the hairdresser was to begin his researches and experiments. Phil Crowe arrived at a cove on the Southern bank of Gullion's lake, a spot supposed to have been where Finn had made his dives from when bathing and swimming there, and near which, it was thought, the poisoned spring might be issuing at the lake's bottom. As he started his researches or experiments he noticed on the other side of the lake certain probing was going on in the water. He had been told that that side of the lake, part of a private estate, had been closed to outsiders, and that the owner had made arrangements with some English chemicals' company to conduct tests on the lake.

Crowe started his tests in a simple way. He had noticed a rat swimming in the lake near the cove, in the very area in which he was interested. He managed to catch the rat, and, on examining its under-parts that had been immersed in the water, he could see no signs that the hair on those parts had been in any way affected by the water.

Of course, he reasoned, the hairs on a rat's belly or under-parts, including the tail, were very short, and the rat's swim had little more than skimmed the surface of the lake. It would require testing in the lake's depth, near the source or entry of the spring. Springs when entering a lake at its bottom, unless shot into strong spurts will disperse at low depths to become diffused in the water around. He would have to make a bigger experiment. He noticed in the valley below several herds of goats. At the time, in many areas of the country, this animal was supplying meat to poor families who could not afford cattle or poultry meat. I remember in my early days in Dundalk there was at least one goat butcher's shop. Its owner was known as the joss butcher. The tenants in the dilapidated hovels in the neighbourhood were numerous enough to have assured him a steady trade.

When the hairdresser chose a goat for his next experiment he was influenced by the fact of the goat's much longer hair than the rat's, and the goat's much greater bulk and weight, a factor likely to bring the goat near the lake's bottom when immersed. When Crowe had purchased a big goat, which he did from one of the small farmers in the neighbouring valley, he was faced with the problem of how he was going to get the live goat into the lake. Goats are notoriously stubborn animals, and they haven't been equipped with tough horns for nothing.

He could, of course, have had a dead goat used in the experiment. But that would not have duplicated what had happened when Finn, after his dive, came in contact with the spring. Finn was a living being at the time; and who knows what the affects of contact would have been had he been a dead body?

As anticipated, getting the goat into the lake proved a difficult task. Crowe had procured a big sack and a net to contain the sack, into which he had put a large stone. The plan was to get the goat into the sack, lower the load deep into the water, then, after an interval when it was judged the animal was still breathing, haul it up again, to examine how its hair had fared. The operation could be repeated.

For the experiment Crowe obviously needed help, and he was able to avail of the services of the farmer who had sold him the goat. After a few attempts at lowering the goat in the water, the farmer got tired, perhaps ashamed of the enterprise. Unable to continue the task himself, Crowe abandoned the experiment, deciding it might be better to await the results of the researches or experiments being attempted at the other side of the lake.

It was now in the middle of the first decade of the new, the Twentieth Century, and much change was to be seen in Dundalk. Where before many of the townsfolk, including some of the prominent among the town fathers, seemed living their lives in pageants, were now involved in new activities, new interests. Two new movements drawing certain measures of support were active in the town. Both had been founded and were being led by women. One was the Irish Women's National Health Association, the other the Women's Suffrage League. The former had something like royal patronage, having as sponsor and activist the wife of His Britanic Majesty's Viceroy in Ireland, the Earl of Aberdeen. And it was probably this sponsorship of the Association had assured it the support of many persons prominent in the business and public life of the town.

The Association had origin in the agitation for better public and private health standards. Much of the ill-health prevalent, made manifest in the spread of tuberculosis and the recurring fever epidemics, had been attributed, at least in part, to the bad sanitary conditions prevalent, particularly in densely populated areas where people were badly housed. Social commentators were writing about Dublin's tenement slums, and its high child mortality rate. Here Dundalk had kindred problems. There were the slums in Wrightson's Lane, Shield's Yard, Squeeze-gut Alley and other hovel places in the town.

The Woman's Suffrage Movement had not gained as large a following in the town as the Health Association. It had not the prestigious patronage the latter was able to attract. However, the Woman's franchise cause had attracted earnest and capable workers, particularly among the leaders in Dublin, one of whom, Hanna Sheehy Skeffington, had visited Dundalk in propagation of the cause.

Both Judge Darleigh and Phil Crowe had become interested in both these movements; and their interest was shown in their attendances at meetings of the bodies. Perhaps not a little of the attraction here for both the judge and the hairdresser was the active involvement in both organisations of Mrs Gráinne Bellew, widow of the but recently deceased, Matthew Bellew, Town Councillor and Poor Law Guardian. Gráinne Bellew was the Gráinne Darragh who, a decade before, had appeared with others, including Phil Crowe, in the cases at the Castletown pageant. There were hints at the time that the remarkable lenience Judge Darleigh had shown the pair had been more than a little influenced by the impression made on him by the good-looking young woman playing the role of Saba. She seemed to have captivated many in the court as well as in the pageant, not just by her looks, but by her grace of movement and the soft tones of her speaking.

For long Algeron Cecil Darleigh had allowed his phobias, including his brooding on his baldness, to keep him isolated from normal social contacts, more particularly with the opposite sex. Now he was finding attraction here that he felt would be harder and harder to resist. He was even thinking of settling down in marriage. Both his parents were dead, and their demise had left him, with his elder bachelor brother, joint heir to the family estate at Ardee.

After the judge's retirement and settling in Dundalk he was to keep note of what was happening to Gráinne Darragh. He had noted how she had become a nurse in the Fever Hospital, in a few years becoming Assistant Matron there, but soon marrying the successful grocer-Town Councillor and Poor Law

Guardian, Bellew, only to be made widow in their first year of marriage. Gráinne Bellew was not one to settle down to anything like retired widowhood. Her nursing experiences in the Fever Hospital had stimulated her interest in public health problems.

Phil Crowe, with whom the retired judge had come more and more in contact, was now in effect the latter's visiting valet, not only attending to shaving and shampooing but rendering general sartorial service. With the judge's greatly awakened interest in social contacts and activities, he had tended to become more venturesome in the matter of dress, more influenced by current trends among townsfolk to be regarded as a person of fashion. The hairdresser-valet was at pains to correct this, determining that ex-Judge Darleigh's wardrobe should keep to the sober cloth of minister grey, in plain, inconspicuous cut. Indeed, it had been commented by observers who had kept an eye on the ex-judge in his promenades in the town that, but for the quality of the cloth he was wearing, its cut and general appearance could well accord with the standards set for the clothing of paupers in the Poor House.

When it came to furnishing Darleigh's wig, for that worthy and most important adjunct or top-dressing, the hairdresser-valet had been more liberal or opulent. It was said to be of the finest facsimile of human hair, its front coils grey, like the legal models, but curling at the back and sides in white quiffs. It could be said the latter accorded well with the pale and ascetic caste of features of the wearer. But the wearer had no doubt that the piece made him much older looking.

Was he beginning to suspect that this was a deliberate and continuing attempt on the part of his barber-valet to make him, Algernon Darleigh, older looking, a natural enough tactic for one who was also a suitor for the favours of the fair widow, Gráinne Bellew? He, his honour, Judge Darleigh, would now be seen on his town strolls with head more poised to his nearly six feet of height, and with gait that all but negatived his lingering limp.

Meanwhile the Women's National Health Association's campaign was rising to something like crescendo. There was much concern in the town about diseases and their transmission through contact with virus-carrying organisms or objects. Mice and rats and even birds, not to talk of small vermin that inhabited offal and dark recesses were now being condemned with vehemence. There were those in the new surge of the health movement ready to go to what others would regard as extremes in combating dreaded infection. These, for example, would have had the town's cats and dogs publicly washed and scrubbed, and its poultry and cage-birds put to something like fumigation at regular intervals. A more thorough extermination of flies, and even of wasps and bees, would have to be undertaken. More attention would have to be paid to wearing apparel. Something would have to be done about women's skirts that trailed the ground. Skirts would have to be shortened, subject of course, to what ecclesiastical authority might say. Some felt strongly that head-wear constituted a danger, coming in contact as it did with the hair, so often the refuge of dangerous organisms.

All these, often hidden, dangers to health came to be discussed at mass meeting in Dundalk's Town Hall, under the auspices of the Women's Health Association's local branch. On the stage were notables from Dublin as well as the local leaders. Notice of the meeting had been displayed prominently in the local press, the *Democrat* and the *Examiner*. The notice stated the meeting would be under distinguished patronage, citing as among the patrons His Honour Judge Algeron Darleigh.

He was present at the meeting, being placed prominently among the important patrons in the front row of the auditorium. Whether he was to address the meeting was not disclosed to the audience, for the meeting was not long going when an incident occurred which was to bring the proceedings to an abrupt end. Mrs Gráinne Bellew, one of the main speakers on the stage, had been warning the audience about the many unsuspected sources or repositories of disease infection which the people generally did not know about or suspect. She dilated on the dangers lurking in wearing apparel, particularly in articles with feather and fur.

To drive home the point, and perhaps set an example for her audience, she advanced to the centre of the stage, took from her neck a feathered boa, an article of apparel then much in fashion, lit a match and set the article alight. Holding it triumphantly aloft, she watched it dissolve in bits of flame and ash on to the stage floor. The action evoked applause, at first muted, but soon rising to greater volume. Then some in the auditorium and a few on the stage, apparently taking the burning of the boa as a signal, started taking articles from their persons and setting them alight. Soon little bonfires were aglow in the hall, which brought the hall attendants to quick action. Fearing the hall and the audience might be in danger of a general conflagration, the attendants ran for buckets of water. Their work was joined by some of the audience with stamping of feet that scattered spark and ash. A general melee ensued, and soon the hall was all but deserted.

The Town Hall authorities soon let it be known the like could not be allowed to occur in their premises again, and the promoters of the meeting, in no way daunted in their efforts to pursue their campaign, decided their next meeting would be really public, would be held in a place where they would be free of the Urban Council's fire restraints. They would hold their meeting in the Market Square, the broad space in the town's centre where general trading took place on market days and where sometimes public meetings were held. That the Court House flanked this place of markets and meetings was hardly a deterrent to any proceedings that might go on in it. The Court House was usually empty of lawyers and police when activities went on in the Square.

So, a month or so after their Town Hall meeting, the promoters and a large crowd assembled in the Market Square. Much of the crowd had been mustered there by the Emmet Band in its parade through the main streets of the town. In the centre of the Square a platform had been erected, and near the platform stood a tall brazier emitting a warm, smokeless glow. The band took up position near the platform. The bandsmen's headdress of black hats in the style of the United Irishmen could hardly have pleased some of the women leaders on the platform. Topping each hat was a large flaunting white feather, which, one would have thought, might have seemed a provocative challenge to campaigners now contending that in the matter of hygienic dress bird plumage was to be strictly avoided.

Among the concourse seen to be entering the Square was Judge Darleigh, given due honour, of course, in the press announcements of his patronage of the Association and its activities. Sight of the uniformed band would probably have reminded the judge of his former pomped entries to the Market Square, when he was attended by escort of cavalry-men flashing sabre and lance. He would probably have remembered his descents from the ornate carriage and his ascent of the steps to the Court's vestibule and reception chamber. He may have remembered that this progress was likely slow, conforming to the dignity the occasion required. He may have pondered how the vast judge's wig he was wearing at the time, its flounces cascading on to his shoulders, causing the wearer perspiration, even fatigue, may have seemed appropriate enough coiffeur for one charged with dispensing British justice, whose principle was: Let justice be done though the Heaven should fall.

But now, in the centre of the square where once sabre and lance flashed, there were glints from a metal brazier as it spluttered and smoked in the early stages of ignition. And some among the crowd assembling were wondering what was the purpose of the embers, which a busy attendant was fuelling and stirring to more ardent glow. The growing flame of the brazier caught the eye of the reminiscing judge, his thoughts perhaps reflecting on past times when fire that burned transgressors at the stake was considered just punishment by the law.

He was aroused from unpleasant reflection by the Chairwoman's announcement for the meeting to begin. The first and main speaker, as at the Town Hall meeting, was Mrs Gráinne Bellew. As before, she stressed the need for attention to hygiene, if the spread of disease in its many forms in the recurring epidemics was to be combated. She enumerated all the sources and substances that fed infection. She laid particular emphasis on wearing apparel, stressing how the seemingly innocent foibles in fashion, fads in feathers and furs, could harbour and help propagate virulent agents of death. Finishing her speech, she descended the platform, in her quick progress shaking, it would seem, almost to flight the clusters of feathers and fur surmounting her hat. It seemed an expensive piece of millinery in the current fashion. With a swaggering air of mixed triumph and disdain, she removed the hat from her head and cast it into the brazier. The hat disappeared in a brief rage of crackling and as brief a burst of multi-coloured flame. Shouts of bravo, and general applause followed. Among the most vociferous here was Phil Crowe. Sure to be of the important in whatever he was actively interested, the hairdresser had been made supervisor of the brazier, looking after its fuelling, registering the discarded for incineration.

Mrs Gráinne Bellew's example was soon followed. Quite a procession of immolators made haste to the brazier, bearing with them all kinds of wearing apparel and haberdashery, notably feather boas and fur-faced muffs, variegated stoles and scarfs.

There was an interval for the raking and re-stoking of the brazier. Suddenly eyes were turned on Judge Darleigh. With his usual dignified step he was walking in the direction of the brazier, one hand engaged in pacing the way with his walking stick, the other holding his large shiny hat. Was he going to consign this expensive-looking piece of headdress to the fire? So far it was only women's hats had been consigned the brazier. Arrived at the brazier he ceremoniously handed his walking stick and hat to the attendant hairdresser. Then, doffing the wig from his head, he cast it into the flames. At the same time he turned his gaze to the platform, anxious to learn the reaction there, particularly of Mrs Gráinne Bellew, to his gesture. He could not but observe the reaction there, an ill concealed titter, soon followed by a chorus of guffaws from the crowd.

The mortified judge seemed rooted to the ground, held there long enough for a swirl of flies to land on his bald pate. He was too wrought to do anything to remove the intruders, these named first in the Association's Index Expurgatorium or Prohibitorium, or, in plain English, the list of pests to be exterminated.

Those at the meeting having some acquaintance with the judge were left wondering why he had publicly divested himself of his wig and exposed his bald head. Was it to impress the widow Gráinne with the measure of his fidelity to the principles she so ardently espoused in advocating the removal from the person of any article of apparel, including head-dress, that might be a breeding place or refuge for disease-carrying vermin? Or was the gesture intended for the hairdresser, a demonstration of the judge's contempt of that over-boastful craftsman's attempt of making a wig?

The answer to such questions was perhaps left in doubt. What was not left in doubt was that neither of these two suitors was to win the hand of the fair widow, Gráinne. She was to marry another successful businessman in the town, an aspirant to membership of the Town Council and Board of Poor Law Guardians.

Chapter 8

In the course of my six weeks stay in Bushy much had happened on the war fronts. The German offensive, begun on the twenty-first of March, when I was wounded early that morning, had succeeded in over-running the British defences that day. For a few weeks the Germans continued their advance, when it seemed the French capital itself might fall to the invaders.

Then there was a turn in the fortunes of the war, when their advance was held and they were forced to retreat. Perhaps it was the coming of the American forces then in greater numbers to succour the Allies that turned the tide. America had entered the war the year before, 1917.

When I was discharged from Bushy to report at Étaples, I was again assigned to the Second-Fifth Battalion of the King's Own Royal Lancaster Regiment. I found the battalion moving in new areas, with the Germans still on the move backwards. We found that those areas had suffered little, at least architecturally, in the German occupation. We found this the case when we entered Arras. There the battalion headquarters, with the officers' mess, kitchen and associated facilities, were established in a well-preserved mansion near the centre of the town. For the cooking staff and officers' servants, as well as for the officers themselves, these new conveniences were a welcome change from the conditions in the trenches, where even the deep and well constructed dugouts were often but a frail defence not only from the artillery and aerial bombardments, but from the assaults of the weather that often sent flooding from the inundated trenches to make muddy puddles on the dugout floor.

This mansion in Arras where we were billeted had a fine library with many books on the French Revolution, several of them on Robespierre, who had been a resident if not native of the town. I had now made sufficient progress in the French language to occupy much of my spare time in reading about events in France leading up to and following the dramatic happenings in 1789. I know of no period in history that presents such a panorama of interesting events and persons.

We were not long in Arras when we were on the move again northwards. It was the Germans in retreat who were determining our movements. When the Germans halted to rally their forces or adjust their positions, pursuers would also have to halt. Naturally the Germans, in their halting places, would go for those with the best defensive features, leaving their pursuers with the more exposed positions. There were still considerable casualties being accounted for on the British side.

With these periodical halts the German retreat went on when, after a few weeks that brought us into early winter, we came to a longer than usual halt near the town of Ath. We had been wondering at the comparative quiet in the line when this morning as many of the ranks as could be mustered in a small field were paraded and brought to attention to hear an announcement by the battalion commander. We were puzzled at the unusual, scrambled way we were assembled. Surprise, not to mention rapturous elation, would be mild terms to describe the reaction of the war-wearied ranks to the commander's announcement that an Armistice was to come into operation at 11 a.m. that day, November 11th, 1918, as a result of agreement between the Allied and enemy forces or governments.

There was such relief at this news that some broke ranks in jubilation and made free from the defence positions. There was still desultory fire from the enemy posts, perhaps in celebration of the impending armistice. As a result there were continuing casualties in the battalion, some of them fatal. Among them, I think was Private Maloney. He had an Irish connection, and did duty in the battalion's sanitary squad.

Later on the day of the Armistice my own rejoicings had an abrupt jolt in a telegram that was delivered to me informing me my mother was seriously ill and suggesting I should apply for leave. I immediately applied to the battalion commander for what was called compassionate leave. The regulations required that before such would be granted the telegram would have to be reported to the authorities in Dublin for its bona fides to be verified by the police there. This took about a week, with the result that when I arrived home I was to find my mother had died and was a few days buried.

My mother's death brought me much sorrow. She had died, I was told, from some growth on the spine, trouble, aggravated by a severe 'flu then causing much illness and death in other parts of Europe as well as in Ireland. Part of the pain at my parent's death was from pangs of conscience over what I was sure were my mother's worries from, firstly, my conflict with the British authorities resulting in my imprisonment, then my involvement in the war.

I felt also for my father, now left to mourn the loss of the mother of their children, the caring consort that had stood by him and then through the many vicissitudes from the bankruptcy of their bakery in Dundalk through the hardships attending unemployment and part-time employment and dependence on charity in a Dublin tenement.

My leave from the battalion, now in Belgium, was for seven days, including the travel days. I was tempted not to return, to desert. But this might have brought unpleasant consequences, with summary arrest and trouble with the authorities again. Besides, there was still much unemployment in the country, including in my own trade, I therefore decided to make the return to the battalion in the prescribed time.

The Germans were now in accelerated retreat towards their own frontier. A few days after I returned the battalion made a ceremonial entry to the town of Ath, where groups of the townsfolk crowded in the streets to hail us with garlands of flowers as welcome deliverers. As in the case of Arras we were to find few signs of the destruction of war in this town, where we were to be billeted for a few weeks. Again the battalion headquarters were to be accommodated in a vacated commodious dwelling. Billeted here we were thus assured of the facilities to cater for the well-being and comfort of the battalion's commissioned officers.

We felt settled in Ath when we were ordered on the go again, this time to the Belgian capital. In Brussels we were assigned a billet with the most suitable facilities or conveniences yet. It was a moderately sized hotel on the edge of a park, a little outside the city, with nearby the important thoroughfare, the Chaussée Waterloo. It had housed a German headquarters before the retreat, and the whole premises, with service essentials, were still intact.

Now military discipline became much relaxed; and with few parades, and with commerce in this fairly large sized city returning to something like normal, life in the billets was rising to more endurable standards. This was paralleled by the widening variety of entertainment available to the troops in the city. I soon became a devotee of the Brussels opera, a municipally controlled enterprise, but availing of foreign vocal talent of high quality. Where before my opera choices were of Verdi 's works and those of the Irish composers, Balfe and Wallace, in the Brussels Theatre La Monnai I became attracted to operas by other composers, especially to Gounod's *Faust* and Gluck's *Orpheus and Eurydice*. I attended performance of the former work so often, I came to whistling to myself practically the whole score from memory.

I found that but few of my colleagues in the battalion were attracted to such entertainment, preferring the more popular kinds of distraction, of which there was plenty of variety in the city. Many of the café's and estaminets had their own entertainers, in some cases vocalists, in others instrumentalists. I remember often going to a small café near the opera house, not so much for its refreshments or comestibles, but to hear a musician. Seated on a raised dais, whether playing or not, he always seemed working himself into contorted positions, perhaps the effects of wounds from the war. He played what I thought an enormous accordion, almost as bulky as himself, and it seemed miraculous how he could handle the multitude of keys with such dexterity and render faultlessly excerpts from *Faust* and other operas and like classical pieces.

I was to meet one British serviceman in my visits to the Brussels opera. I had been on nodding acquaintance with him before in his periodic visits to our billet. He was a corporal in the military police or redcaps. He would be on his rounds of inspection, and, sometime accompanied by a colleague, perhaps his sergeant, he would look round our billet in the hotel, tarrying in the officers' mess and in the kitchen, when the head cook would permit him sample some of the delicacies, and even the wines being made ready for the officers' dinner. Even in these reaches of the battalion headquarters one had to keep the police on one's side.

I got to know this Police Corporal Tracey when by accident I found myself seated next to him in the Brussels opera. He proved to be a keen opera lover and could talk eloquently about his favourite pieces. Quite loquacious, in the intervals in the bar he talked freely of his own history. He had been born and brought up in Liverpool, both his grandparents being of Irish origin. He was married, his wife being also of Irish origin.

Corporal Tracey had been a prison warder in England before his conscription into the Army in 1916. He was in his early thirties. Around middle height, broad of chest and sturdy of limbs, he seemingly had the physique for law enforcement. But his face, though flaunting a bristling moustache of sandy hair, had a mobility that could quickly alternate between the raising of eyebrows in conjecture or surprise to the more positive delineation of smiles wreathing the mouth.

Later in the theatre bar we were discussing the performance of *Faust*. The Corporal was particularly impressed by the soprano and dilated much on her rendering of the Jewel song, in that scene in which she fondles jewels she draws from a casket, imagining them gracing her person. After the performance we visited that café nearby where the highly skilled accordionist was performing. His repertoire included the *Faust* pieces which prompted the corporal to dilate again on the soprano's rendering of the Jewel song. He stopped suddenly and drew from an inside pocket a small brown box or casket. Opening it he displayed a rosary beads, the beads small, but glinting with some kind of inlaid jewels. The crucifix was similarly inlaid. The whole made quite a glitter in the velvet-lined casket.

Corporal Tracey was quite obviously proud of what he must have regarded as a treasure. He went on to explain he had bought the expensive article as a birthday present for his wife. Her birthday would be in a few months time, when he hoped, the war now over, he would be able to get home leave and so be in Liverpool for the celebration. He explained that his spouse, being a very religious woman, this was the most appropriate gift he could take to her. As for himself he tried to practise his religion, that also of the Roman Catholic persuasion, as best he could in the difficult war situation. He hoped now with the armistice he would be able to resume the normal practise of his religion.

It was now late on this night as we left the café, destined, as I thought, for our respective billets, when he surprised me, perhaps shocked me would be the better term, when he asked me if I would like to visit a brothel, not an ordinary brothel, he explained, but one of quality. After some moments, my astonishment now easing, and my curiosity stirred, I agreed to accompany the corporal. Now a few months domiciled in this city of Brussels, I could not but have heard of its brothel area, its red-light district. It was known to have its patrons not only in the battalion, but in other units of the British Army in the city. There was talk of its being a source of a current spread of venereal disease. It was not that there was much alarm about that apparent in the battalion. Indeed, there was much levity about the disease; in some cases it being regarded as a matter to boast about, to be taken as a sign of one's virility.

The brothel district was only a few moments walk from the Opera House and my favourite café. We entered a narrow street, with half a dozen or so three-storey dwelling-like houses on each side of it. It was ill lit except for some of the windows on the ground-floors of the houses. These were lighted enough to display the charms of young women seated in their sitting rooms, projecting enticement to the passers-by in the street.

The corporal led our hurried exit from this thoroughfare into a small square. Here the houses were fewer, more commodious and affluent looking. Approaching one of them, we were greeted politely by a porter. He was dressed in heavy livery that, festooned with big brass buttons, gave emphasis to his sturdy and athletic physique. The corporal led our entrance, to the porter's respectful address: 'M'sieu' le Corporal'. This salutation to us was to be repeated by other members of the establishment during our visit there.

With the corporal thus monopolising the greetings or courtesies, I was quite content to remain in tandem as it were, with the one in front taking the salutations. It was obvious the corporal was well known in the place.

When we were ushered inside we were led to a large apartment, where on a stage at the end something like a dramatic entertainment was going on. All on the stage were young women, in their twenties or early thirties. All of them were scantily dressed, except one, who, from what one could see of her face, seemed to have the most attractive features of any of them. She was dressed in a nun's habit; and the only dramatic action we were to see was her being divested gradually of her clothes till she stood naked. She was then pinioned and subjected to whipping, the whips scourging her body seeming to be of leather thongs. Yet though handled with vigour, they were leaving no marks on the defrocked nun. The whipping operations were performed in turn by her co-performers on the stage.

We were scarcely entertained by the crude performance; and in taking the lead in our exit from the spectacle the corporal uttered strong criticism of what he angrily termed a brazen insult to decency as well as to religion. We then found ourselves in another large apartment, a well-furnished one like a lounge in a luxury hotel. Indeed it was more like an old-fashioned drawing-room, save that there were many short tables set in it, which in the milieu of baroque furniture, tapestries and chandeliers, suggested the profanity of commerce.

There were tables each with two well-upholstered chairs. Other tables were larger with chairs to accommodate four persons. My companion chose one of the latter tables, leaving me wondering if he was expecting or procuring company. There were several other men in the room, some of them with women, the latter obviously of the house. We were the only men in the place in service uniforms; and when I seemed to be pondering on this in my survey of the room, my companion informed me that some of the men I had observed were in fact servicemen in mufti, civilian-dress. These were commissioned officers, who preferred to take their leisure or diversions without the habiliments of their rank or their regiment. The corporal went on to explain that there might be among them a few higher non-commissioned officers whose pay would permit of their coming to such a place to be entertained. Some of the lower rank non-commissioned officers might manage by saving up their service pay perhaps for months. He, the corporal, being of the police, had more or less free entry.

The waitresses serving the patrons at the tables seemed of the company we saw on the stage in the other apartment. They seemed to have added somewhat to their wearing apparel, but still with sight of flesh and gesture made plain their calling. We noticed one of these young women we had seen on the stage loitering near our table, when she would alternate her stare between the corporal and the empty chair near him. To my surprise the corporal seemed disposed to join her in the exercise and soon the exchange of stares brought her to our table where she seated herself on the chair near the corporal. The corporal seemed to have plenty of money, and had insisted on paying for my drinks as well as for his own during the night. He now included our lady companion in his orders.

Our companion turned out to be the lady who acted as the nun in the stage piece. She looked none the worst for the defrocking and whipping she had undergone on the stage. Soon our conversation developed into a tête-à-tête between the corporal and herself; as they moved chairs nearer to one another. They spoke in a kind of French, perhaps part Flemish, which may have been the lingo of the local underworld, but of which I understood little. By now I felt in effect excluded from the conversation, when suddenly the two of them got to their feet, she edging out towards the door that opened to the more private or reserved part of the house. The corporal turned to me, I thought, to explain this sudden turn, which, indeed, he did by laying on my lap his red-cap and his cane, apparently to mind for him. Then, bracing himself for what he no doubt thought a more serious or solemn commission, he drew from an inner pocket the little brown case with the rosary beads. Handing me this further article, in hushed tones he asked me to look after these pieces of his belongings, saying he would be back in fifteen minutes.

He then moved quickly towards the door, kept ajar for him by the lady that had briefly honoured us with her company. I thought, he would be absent for fifteen minutes. Was this the unit of accountancy in the establishment? And what was the charge in excess of that? - overtime rate presumably. Why did I move the corporal's red-cap and silver-knobbed cane to the table before me? Surely it wasn't to make known to all present, patrons and staff, that I had been invested with these symbols of law and authority? What a change that might have seemed in the fortunes of one that had defied that law and authority

It turned out the corporal was as good as his word, returning to our table after fifteen minutes. He was grateful for my having looked after his property during his absence. Curious to know something about his adventures in the interior, presumably upstairs in the chambers where I assumed the main business of the establishment was transacted, I remarked to him it was just as well he had committed to me custody of his belongings, particularly the holy gift intended for his wife. I hinted, did he not think it something of a profanity bringing the like into such a place? He smiled, to inform me that the bedroom he had been in had on its walls several holy pictures. He went on to tell me that all the bedrooms in the place had tokens of religion in them, and that an alcove to the rooms bore a shrine to Our Lady, the Blessed Virgin, with statue, candles and vases of flowers. It was evident he was a regular patron of the place, that his visits were not just concerned with police inspection or supervision.

It was now late, nearing midnight, and on our way out of the place, in the vestibule we met again the door porter. Near him hovered a portly dame, her figure, in contrast with the much younger women seen in the house, sumptuously as well as respectably dressed. But, above the chaste neck-line of the toilette, and under the hennaed coiffure, its pomps of curls braced with ill-concealed padding, glowed the lady's face, a battle map, its tints revealing, rather than concealing, the advance of the enemy years.

This was the directress or madame of the establishment. With her, emphasising contrast, stood the stripling who had acted the role of the nun in the stage presentation and later filled the role of quarter-hour consort of the corporal. With the doorman, the trio had assembled in the vestibule to see us off. They repeated their *au revoirs* with an air of confidence that we'd soon be back.

The next morning at my duties in the kitchen I found it hard to concentrate on the work, so much was my mind occupied with the happenings of the night before. Later in off-duty interval I thought to turn my thoughts from the preoccupation by scanning one of the local newspapers. It was a daily I sometimes read to acquaint myself with current affairs, the while, I hoped, improving my knowledge of French. Looking over the news items I came across a report that the British Military Police in the city had for some days past been investigating a break-in and robbery, in which it was suspected some members of the British forces in the city were involved. The premises concerned belonged to a firm of jewellers in the city's centre. Among the comprehensive range of the firm's stock were varieties of ecclesiastical requisites, chalices, monstrances, crosiers, crucifixes, candelabras, vases, rosary beads. Was this the source of the gift the corporal was keeping for his wife?

At this time we had but a few more days before the end of our posting in Brussels. So we were not to hear anything more of the case or of Corporal Tracey. One of the remaining nights I thought to spend at the opera. Again it was *Faust*, and in the interval in the bar, quaffing a beer, I thought of the corporal, conjuring him there dilating on the Jewel song, his fervour agitating the glass of beer in his hand, stirring its froth to effervescence of beads.

We were well into the spring of a New Year, 1919 when the battalion left Brussels to join the Army of Occupation in Germany.

En route our first stop was in the city of Cologne. Our halt there brought us near the cathedral. We noticed there was scaffolding round parts of it, and assumed this was as a result of damage done the edifice by Allied bombing. This was not the case. We were to learn that scaffolding on the building, at one part or another, had been a permanent or continuing feature, as over the centuries back to the middle ages generations of building craftsmen had been working on the building, doing repairs and alterations. This could strike one as a fine bit of labour history in itself. But though the cathedral struck me as an impressive mass of the architect's and builder's arts, I was drawn more to what I had seen of French and Belgian church and other public building architecture, and to what I had observed in pictures of similar buildings in Italy.

We went from Cologne southwards to Euskirchen, another town in the Rhine Valley, and the battalion headquarters staff became billeted in a village, a dozen or so miles from the town. It was more a townland of scattered domiciles of the small farm kind, at what seemed its centre being a small hotel that probably found trade only from tourists come to fish or hunt, or perhaps just to rest in the rustic landscape of the place.

The battalion headquarters took up occupation of the hotel. It was not yet the tourist season, and the occupation was content to allow the proprietor, Herr Busche and a few of his staff accommodation in part of the hotel. With the kitchen and mess staff accommodated in serviceable apartments, it was not long till I made the acquaintance of Herr Busche and one of his staff, a housemaid, Fraulein Guttmann. Herr Busche spoke a kind of guttural French probably learned from tourists before the war, but we were able to converse haltingly. He was a soft-mannered and suave man, determined obviously to get on with the occupation authorities as well as he could. I wanted more to become acquainted with his maid. Mariechen Guttmann spoke a little of the French spoken by her master, with the same intonation and attempts at colloquialisms. When I had learned in Brussels of our impending despatch to Germany I procured myself an English-German grammar, and with this I started working with Mariechen to learn some of her native language. Our sessions were mostly furtive, at guarded intervals, in out of the way recesses, for it had to be remembered I was of the occupation, and she of a people that up to recently had been at war with the Allies.

Mariechen was perhaps a few years older than myself, of rather plain but kindly looks. She had at least that charm which I suppose most foreigners have for us, at least when we are young. I felt our language liaison was beginning to engender something like romantic overtones when Mariechen announced plans for her early departure to a new post in Cologne. Perhaps someone of the surveillance had decided my liaison with the Fraulein was not in accord with the spirit of the occupation.

I had a liaison of another kind at the same time, and again with a foreigner. It was one of friendship but of a kind that under tests could dissolve into its opposite. Private Edmond Lombardi was an officer's servant who acted as waiter in the officers' mess of our hotel billet. He was a native of the South of France, likely of Italian extraction. At the outbreak of the war he was domiciled in London where he worked as waiter in one of the principal hotels there. To watch Edmond serve at table was to learn that waiting could be much more than a menial or servile occupation. He was noticeably erect at around five foot and three-quarters, perhaps a slight bit round-shouldered, but with a command of his arms that could wield his elbows in easy axels, so that he was able to handle or manipulate dishes in trajectories round the heads of seated guests without seeming in any way to invade their conversations or confidences. It seemed like the performance of a conjurer or juggler.

I was not surprised when I found Lombardi had had some gymnastic experience, and that his skill and grace of movement had been acquired, at least partly, at boxing and wrestling practice, sports in which I myself had an interest and some practice. Before we engaged together in these recreations in a contrived gymnasium in the hotel billet we had already established companionable relations in discussing matters of common interest. For conversational purposes his English was better than my French, for he had been schooled for high-class hotel work, and had had a few years experience in the trade in England. We shared tastes in the arts, particularly in music. He spoke much of the opera house in his native Nice, describing the operas he had attended there and claiming some of the performances were the equal in standard of the performances in Paris or Milan. He had little enthusiasm for the army, whilst hardly sharing my political objections to being conscripted into it. He longed, like myself, for the occupation to be over, when, he hoped to become settled in his own trade in his own country.

We had made almost a daily exercise of practice in the billet's gymnasium.

We had sessions with boxing-gloves, usually both of us concentrating on the evasive or defensive aspect of the sport. Whilst unspoken about it, we both wanted to remain friends and avoid anything of the aggressive side of the sport. But this day, without any deliberations by either of us, at least at the start, we gradually passed from purely defensive sparing and feinting and blocking into more aggressive action till suddenly, as if by mutual consent, we stopped boxing, when I am sure each of us discarded the boxing gloves more with disgust than with any other feeling. I am sure he felt my feeling of estrangement now, both of us to ponder how bonds of mutual interest and regard or sympathy can be pierced by that demon instinct to prevail or dominate.

With little other activities than the routine military duties to occupy one I took to exploring the countryside in the vicinity of our hotel billets. It was a valley landscape of small farms with a river, a tributary of the Rhine winding through and seeming to come from a range of hills bordering its Northern bank. From when I first saw this landscape it reminded me strongly of that rural retreat a mile or so West of Dundalk's outer reaches, Toberona. The name is Gaelic for John's Well. The area is flat land, most of which is divided by hedges into small farms, each with its cottage dwelling and outhouses, these latter in most cases probably housing a few cattle and poultry. The Castletown River runs through the middle of this landscape, and as marking the centre of the scene a rough stone bridge spans the river.

Probably what brought Toberona so much to mind in surveying this Rhineland scene was the Spring verdure of primroses, hawthorn and laburnum that suffused the latter's ditches and hedges. It was a like prospect that endeared me with Toberona when I first visited when a schoolboy accompanied by my father.

As well as having this rustic and restful scenery, Toberona had cultural traditions. Up to the early part of the nineteenth century a pattern or fair annually celebrated Saint John's Day, 24th June, when well-known bards and other artists from Louth and surrounding counties would gather in the vicinity of Toberona bridge, to show their talents. It is recorded that over-indulgence in alcohol and rowdying brought an end to the patterns.

When our bakery was going in Dundalk my father was a frequent visitor to Toberona. His main attraction there was the home of the bakery yard-man. Pat Quigley, with wife and small family, lived in one of the cottages in Toberona, and his outhouses housed a few pigs as well as cattle and poultry. It might be asked how my father found congenial the company of the yardman, an employee of the bakery. It was hardly strange, though, considering the origin of our bakery. My father had worked in the same bakery as Quigley, my father having been apprenticed there as a baker, Quigley working there as a yardman.

At the time the conditions of work in Messrs McCann's, the principal bakery in Dundalk, were very hard, the bakery operatives having to work at night, with long working hours, sometimes around a hundred hours a week. Most of the bakers were in the local trade union, known as the Dundalk Bakers' Society.

My father was then President of the Society, and he had written a poem rallying support for a strike which the bakers had embarked on in attempt to right their grievances. As expressing some of the irksome conditions and the spirit of the strikers, excerpts from my father's verses may be quoted:

Awake! arise to freedom's call!
You men who over-toil,
And cast aside that yoke of gall
Which long did round you coil
Your hours of labour now shall be
But ten in twenty-four -
Get ready, then, stand up like men,
And we'll be slaves no more.

The Poor House and the early grave
Have been the end for long
Of many a weary brother slave
Who sank beneath his wrong.
Whilst others, too, have passed away
'Ere manhood days were o'er,
And sank beneath the tyrants sway
To be their slaves no more.

And when the Sunday morning dawns
And bells ring out for prayer,
The baker cannot go to church,
He has no time to spare,
What matter if his soul be lost
The work must go before.
We'll put that down, what 'er the cost,
And be their slaves no more.

The verses concluded with a call for united action. Not all the bakers responded to the strike call, and only one of the yard and transport workers of the bakery joined the strike. That was Pat Quigley, but some said of him that he had this small farm out in Toberona and that would well sustain him. My father and the other union leaders appreciated Quigley's support in an action that was but partly successful. And after the strike when the three leaders, my father, John Cooper and James Reilly, started their own bakery, they employed Pat Quigley as yardman, in charge of the bread vans and the stabling of the horses.

The strike in McCann's occurred in 1890. It was the following year, the partners of the new bakery, the strike leaders, opened their business near the town's centre, in Clanbrassil Street. This was the year of Parnell's death, an event that did little to lessen the political ferment following the scandal that involved the leader. For the whole decade and into the next faction rancour was to dominate politics in Dundalk and the whole North Louth constituency.

My father was a partisan in this, being a firm Parnellite. His two trade or business partners differed with him here, their political attitudes being influenced more by the partisanship of the Church spokesmen in the Parnell controversy. However, in these early days of the new bakery its business seemed to prosper. Good trade was developing, not only in the town but in wide areas around. Several delivery vans were now on the road, and Quigley, the yardman, had persuaded the management to furnish more stabling.

In fact, at this time my father, it would seem, was coming more and more under the influence of the yardman. He was paying visits to Quigley's home in Toberona. My father, of course, had been drawn to the yardman by the latter's support of the strike in McCann's; but, apart from that, there were some mutual interests which they shared. Music was a strong one. The yardman was a member of the Emmet Band, being an accomplished player of the clarinet. My father, as well as being a fairly good baritone singer, played the violin fairly well and could render a range of good tunes on the harp. My father's visits to Quigley's home developed to bringing his violin with him when, accompanied by the yard-man on the clarinet, they would discourse Moore's melodies and excerpts from the operas.

I don't know if my father could have traced his ancestry beyond his father and mother. His father had died young. My father knew he had been a baker in Dublin, where the family then lived. On his death, the widow, with three children, including my father, came to Dundalk, apparently the widow's home town. Here, probably at a very early age, he became an apprentice in McCann's bakery. He could have had little school education. But, endowed with considerable talent, he succeeded in educating himself to becoming well read and attaining to some facility in verse-writing, and even in music-composition as well as music-playing.

The yardman also had scant school education, but inherent talents had acquired him many practical skills, which he had demonstrated in small farm building and management. It seemed somewhat incongruous that he shared my father's musical tastes. A big man physically, with body and limbs well attuned to hard physical labour, he seemed out of real character, indeed, almost matronly, in the encomiums he was in the habit of lavishing on my father. He would praise the verse and the lyrics my father composed, I am sure much beyond their merit, claiming that their author should have been acknowledged as a second Thomas Moore or Oliver Goldsmith.

The drink orgies that had marked and put an end to the patterns of the bards and poets in Toberona had their memorials in the surviving illicit domestic brewing and distilling secretly operated in some of the Toberona hamlets. This represented one of the skills acquired by the apt yardman, and his brand of poteen had the reputation among the select visitors to his dwelling of being the equal of good, matured malt whiskey.

But legend had it Toberona did not require either brewed or distilled liquor to engender anything like transports of inebriation. Toberona had its well of spring water, named after Saint John, and those quaffing of its draughts, if endowed to even the slightest extent with poetic or rhetorical talent, would be inspired to speech worthy of the most gifted orator or author. They had a saying in The Temple tavern: Tell it in Toberona!

This was a judgement admonition by The Templars when they felt bored by some habitué over-pedestrian or dreary in narrative or commentary. The more sophisticated Templars would be impatient with the merely literal or prosaic.

They would hold that imagination was not just concerned with will-o-the-wisp fantasy, but is often the source, nay, the begetter of truth. And what of exaggeration? My father would have said, in effect: We have only to harken how the world condemns or praises to realise that exaggeration is the great revealer of the truth.

Our bakery was doing well for a few years when there was a turn in the trade. One of the partners broke from the partnership to open a bakery for himself at the lower end of the street. It was James Reilly, who differed with his colleague partners on the role of machinery in the bakery trade. My father, and the other partner, John Cooper, wanted to keep to the old handcraft methods, believing the old processes produced better-eating and better-looking bread. A certain amount of mechanisation had been introduced in the trade in Britain and the North of Ireland. It had increased productivity and reduced costs. The ex-partner, Reilly, had now installed machinery in his bakery and was selling his products cheaper than ours in trading in the town and surrounding areas.

It was not long until this competition had its effect on our bakery's trade. But my father instead of adapting to the mechanisation changes remained stubbornly committed to the older methods, with the result our bakery's business gradually declined. My father's objections to machinery was not merely that it would affect the quality, more particularly in the matter of the flavour, of the bread, but that it would put bakers out of employment. Originally his plans for the bakery were that it should be run on co-operative lines, with the workers having a say as well as shares in its running. The partners had started the bakery with partly their own subscribed capital and partly capital put up by friends sympathetic to the project. But, the bakery started, my father found both his partners, Reilly and Cooper, unsympathetic to the co-operative idea, and the bakery just went on running on ordinary commercial lines.

After what he regarded as the defection of his partner Reilly, and the decline in our bakery's trade, my father, instead of trying to re-adjust to the situation in some practical way, went into long pondering and expostulating on what co-operation would have meant in the running of the bakery. These bouts of cogitation and lamentation were extended in more frequent visits to The Temple and to the Quigley home in Toberona. The visits to Toberona and the returns were now being made in Tommy Hearty's hackney car, or, as romantic ballads described the vehicle, his jaunting car. Tommy Hearty and his jaunting car found a congenial milieu in this region of the Quigley home. He was known as the Man with the Gun, one of the local Invincibles, the heirs of the Fenian Brotherhood.

With the talk and liquor in Quigley's merging fantasies could be woven by such as my father and the car driver. Indeed, in Toberona it would be natural to conjure scenes and happenings of magic. Was it not the Cuchulainn and Finn Mac Cool country, the plain whose sward had given paddock and pasture to the Fianna, and grazing, in gift or tribute, to Maeve's cattle? Did not its northern edge extend into the shadow of Slieve Gullion, the great hill that reared its lake aloft as if to catch the dew of the early morning, or reared to mirror the eerie dance of lark ascending?

Though my mother was generally tolerant of my father's convivial evenings with his associates, she baulked at his visits to Toberona. She had come to mistrust the yardman and his flattery of my father. She regarded my father as too trusting, too high-minded, too much of an idealist to put up with such an associate as Quigley. True, she had got him to put a cement surface on the yard of our home, designed to rid the yard of Aunt Mary's hens, the feathered proletariat that dared strut at our mahogany hall-door.

The transfer of the poultry to Quigley's domain, where they were now being fed largely on stable offal, had brought a falling-off of eggs in our household, with the disposal of some of them to customers of the yardman. Further, my mother's informant had discovered that following the withdrawal from their routes of two of the bakery's bread-vans and the disposal of their horses, consequent on the shrinking of trade, the yard-man was now letting out the vacant stables to casual callers at the yard, country visitors come to town for business. They would unyoke horse from cart, or pony from trap, leaving the vehicles in the yard and the beasts to be stabled by the yardman. The fodder he would furnish would be the property of the bakery, but payment for it went to the yardman, as well as charge for looking after the vehicle and stabling the animal.

Such abuses had been going on a considerable time before being known by my father and his business partner, John Cooper, the latter being more concerned with the actual bakehouse production than with the business management. My mother came to believing that the yardman was soothsaying my father with flattery and encouragement to liquor indulgence for the purpose of running the concern into bankruptcy, and perhaps in consort with some monied acquaintances acquiring it. My mother now spoke of Quigley as a snake in the garden of innocence my father laboured to cultivate, the snake's fangs oozing their toxin through honeyed tongue.

It was said that at times the yardman had extended the illicit stabling to furnishing lodgings to the man with the bear, the itinerant with his shaggy mate now making so frequent visits to the town, they were all but permanent residents. There was a story of a visit paid the yard one morning by a Miss McShane, a spinster of advancing years who kept a shebeen, masked as a tea and confectionery and mineral refreshments, situated near our bakery. She had entered the yard to make customary purchase of eggs from the yardman. She liked her eggs fresh or new-laid and was given run of the stables to collect her half-dozen, sure, as if confirmed by the clucking hens, that her eggs were fresh. This morning, unaware of its occupation by the bear, she had entered a stable, and instead of hearing hen cackle, she heard the deep growl of the bear. Startled and nearly paralysed with fear, she panicked from the stable, fearing pursuit and perhaps mauling or crushing by the bear. After, there was a joke in the town that the lady had reached old age without ever having attracted embrace by a man or even by a bear.

Chapter 9

These reveries of Toberona and my native town were cut short by the Mess Corporal informing me he had word that I was to be sent to hospital in Euskirchen. I had been complaining of pain and swelling in my left arm and hand and had been given light duties in the kitchen. The headquarters M.O. had said it was a suppuration of the shrapnel wounds I suffered at the opening of the German offensive the previous year. My most unpleasant experience in the Euskirchen hospital, where I had a two-weeks' stay was the removal of the thumb nail from my left hand without anaesthetic. I did not know if this was a consequence of the war's exhaustion of medical requisites, or whether it was in conformity with the hospital authorities view or requirement that patients sent to the hospital by the occupation power should have the fortitude to bear their aches without recourse to the concoctions of pain avoidance.

When I left the Euskirchen hospital Summer was well advanced, and the signs of the advance were much the same, - I thought, as I would have experienced in Toberona were I there now, were I there to see the changes in its fields and hedges; in the fields the ripening corn and the meadow flowers that manage to thrive in the press of hardy weeds and harder stone; and in the hedges, the wild roses and honeysuckle that scramble with briars soon to be drooped with the mellowed fruit of the blackberry. And above the tangles of briars would be the laburnum trees that reluctantly had raised their boughs above the hedges to droop them hedgewards, their earlier golden petals now wilted to blanched stalks. And, still higher than the laburnums, would be the chestnut trees, their former festoons of bloom now wrought into mahogany polished nuts, in green, spiked casques, again to be dowered on hedge and ditch.

My cogitations on the recollected Toberona scene now duplicated in the Rhine Valley were now dispelled by the news that the battalion was to prepare for departure from Germany for some destination in Britain, and demobilisation there. There was among all ranks in the battalion all but universal rejoicing at the news. The regimen of keeping aloof from the Germans, and the unfamiliarity with their language, had for most in the occupation much the character of exile.

It turned out the battalion's homeward destination was not to be in Britain but in my own country. We landed in the Curragh Camp in a fine Autumn day in September. Whilst abroad we had heard little or nothing about the guerrilla forays of the Republican forces now being reported in the country. The armed raids and ambushes at this stage were sporadic, and seemed not widely enough operated or organised to suggest anything like a revolution might be in prospect.

Demobilisation was quickly effected in the Curragh, military uniforms discarded for supplied civilian attire. The dispersal sent travel to domiciles in many parts of the British Isles, with only myself left on native ground. I made haste for reunion with my father, and my brother and my sister, and my Aunt Mary and her husband, John Cooper, my father's former business partner. Though still, with Cooper, working as journeyman baker, in one of Kennedy's bakeries in the city, my father seemed to have aged a lot. I thought no doubt my mother's death the previous November was a factor here. My brother was working for a boot-and-shoe salesman in a busy business not far from our home. My invalid sister was still domiciled with the Coopers, who had no children of their own. As in Dundalk we still had associations with the Clanbrassil Clan, our home, an upstairs flat in a row of recently built houses, was in a short, narrow street, formerly known as Dowker's Lane, but now titled Clanbrassil Terrace.

Since my spell in the hospital in Germany I had worried whether I would be able ever to work at my trade again. My left arm and hand had been partly incapacitated with the wounds. There was still much hard manual work in the bakery trade. In the army kitchens since being wounded I had been given light work. Such would not seem a possibility, were I to succeed in finding work in a Dublin bakery. At the same time I did not want to be an encumbrance on my father and my brother. At demobilisation some of us who had worked in army kitchens were offered jobs in a civilian organisation that operated under army authority catering for army personnel in areas where they were quartered. After demobilisation, given eight shillings a week disability pension, and work at my trade in Dublin not being available to me, I took the job in the canteen offered me, and I was assigned to a bakery in the Curragh. There I worked as a confectioner, being spared heavy handling of materials or other onerous work by a co-operative staff. After some months there I was transferred to the organisation's establishment in Belfast. With this practise I found the wounded limb gradually recovering something like normal functioning, and eventually felt I should now be fit to work again at my trade in Dublin.

I found, though, that the trade in Dublin was slack, with many bakers and confectioners unemployed, some of them getting odd days at casual work. At the same time I was not able to settle at work for the canteens. I wanted to be away from any association with the British Army. My father shared my feelings on this, and we were both agreed I should end this particular association without delay. I also voluntarily gave up the army disability pension, regarding this as an undesirable link better severed. This now meant signing on at the Dublin Labour Exchange to draw unemployment benefit. After a few weeks drawing benefit I, with a few others, was offered work by the exchange, the work being in the building trade on sites in France. I had become friendly with another unemployed person whom I had met at band recitals in St. Stephen's Green in the city. He shared my tastes in good music and himself was a competent musician on the flute. We took the jobs on offer by a building contractor operating in Paris.

We travelled there to find the work was on a building site, on which, with our labour, was to rise to what was to become the well-known department store, Au Printempts. Both Vincent Hyland and myself had hoped, along with finding work in the French capital, to have profited also by improving our speaking knowledge of the French language. We found our hopes of the latter were hardly justified. Many of our workmates on the site were foreigners, Lascars, and the native French work colleagues were largely uneducated and spoke a patois we found it hard to understand.

Our wages were poor, and we could ill-afford to go to the Grande Opera or to other similarly high-class entertainment. But we found there is much of cultural interest in Paris that may be availed of or enjoyed with little or nothing to pay. There are museums and galleries of different kinds, and even some of the city's cemeteries will be found with cultural and historical interest. We were to spend hours on a few Sundays in Père Lachaise Cemetery, which was not far from our lodging in the Clichy district. In Père Lachaise Cemetery many of the tombs themselves were of artistic interest, the sculptor's art rising above the almost ubiquitous model of the cross seen in our cemeteries. Père Lachaise had illustrious tenants to honour, including our own Oscar Wilde. I was a stonemason's helper at the building of Au Printempts. When we progressed to work on the third floor I became subject to attacks of giddiness, or vertigo. I tried to fight it and became quite ill, eventually having to be sent to hospital, an institution in Paris catering mostly for British and American residents in the city. After a couple of weeks stay in the hospital I felt little better and, feeling not fit enough to resume work at the building site, I returned to Dublin.

But I was feeling more confident I would soon be able to work at the bakery trade again. In anticipation of this I made application to rejoin the union. During my stay in London and my detention by the British Army my former membership of the union had lapsed, and I thought now, with the unemployment reported in the trade it might be a considerable time before the union could grant me re-admission.

They were times of much change and trouble. The Treaty with Britain and the Provisional Government came in the early 1920s, the Civil War in 1922-23. It was in the former year, whilst the conflict was still on, that I had gone to work in Paris. I succeeded in having my membership of the union re-established in 1924. In the interval of several months before that I had depended on my father for support. That was given without complaint. Indeed, he indulged me to the extent that he was advising me not to worry about delay in getting back to my trade but to explore the prospects of trying to establish myself as a writer. He suggested I write articles and submit them to some of the popular press. He understood a certain newspaper was paying well for accepted articles. At the back of the terrace where we lived there was a big scrap-yard, where were piled discarded articles, mostly of the rusted machinery kind. It could be seen in some detail from our upstairs flat. My father suggested I write an article about it. I did, and sent it to the *Irish Independent*, a daily newspaper then reputed to have the largest circulation of the native daily periodicals. The article was published, and I was duly paid for it. I am not sure whether the fee paid was a guinea-and-a-half or three guineas. My father rejoiced over this, and suggested I should adopt as a literary signature to my writings the name John Deane Swift. My father was inspired in this in the fact that my mother's maiden or family name was Deane. I preferred to think my father was motivated in this by the idea that my mother should also be a recipient in whatever acclaim or honour my writings should earn. That was preferable to his imagining there was honour or honours for me in associating my name with the celebrated Dean of Saint Patrick's.

I no longer remember how I wrote about that scrap-yard with its heaps of old and rusted vehicles and other machines; but I do know my father would have liked that I stressed how the like, when working, had probably harmed handcraft and put workmen out of jobs. The success I had with the article had not encouraged me to attempt any further literary efforts aimed at publication in newspapers. Certainly I would not attempt anything for submission to the *Irish Independent*. I had got to know that at the time of the British authorities' suppression of the 1916 Rebellion that periodical called for the execution of James Connolly.

My father had long thought I should have taken more seriously to writing. He had known I had some aptitude for composition when I was at school. But he was quite critical of my efforts in this item of my schooling, an example was a school essay, or rather description I wrote of a trade exhibition that was held in the Dundalk Athletic Grounds. He thought it was too literal, that a reporter without imagination might have written. I had described the more important things in the exhibition. He criticised that I should have had living beings, people, in my account, and, in writing of people, imagination. Imagination, he claimed, should always be used. He conceived poetic license as a right accorded not just the poet but the writer or writers who might write about the poet, or, indeed, about anyone else.

My father went on to advise that instead of writing compositions, as per school requirements, on such subjects as a sojourn in the country, or a train journey to Dublin, I should be writing about him or my mother or the Aunt Mary. He would add I should not be bound to the literal or photographic, since imagination was the great portrayer, the great recorder. My father would say, in effect, we could leave it to that often beknighted class, the unimaginative or literalist to criticise those who could see truth or logic even in the absurd or the fatuous.

I had left school and, in a sense, had become a professional writer, in the meaning that I was now employed scripting legal documents in the office of the County Louth Crown Solicitor. True, my wages were only two shillings and six-pence per week; but, then, there was the prestige thought much of at the time of working at the law.

One day in the office, perhaps bored copying documents in a tedious court case, I began, covertly, of course, and in disjointed notes, writing about my father. I had heard enough about him, of events in his earlier days to give something like verisimilitude or authenticity to what I was writing. I wrote of him as of twenty or so years earlier when the trade in which he worked was experiencing radical changes. He was working in McCann's bakery when the management decided the dough-making process should be done by machinery, instead of by hand, as was the practice before. Another change effected at the time was that the fermenting agent to be used in the dough making should henceforth be the newly patented substance, yeast. Up to this the fermenting agent used in the firm, as in the trade generally, was a brew or distillation made of hops. The brewing or distilling process was done in the bakery; and it was held baker's reputed fondness for alcoholic beverages was due, not so much to assuaging thirst induced by heat in the bakehouse but through habit of sampling the potency of the brew, the manufacture of which was then a normal part of bakehouse work.

My father was put in charge of the machine, the firm's dough-maker, a position remunerated above the ordinary bakery operative. Some suggested this charge was rather a penalty imposed on him by the firm, on account of his known views critical of machinery in the trade and the active role he was then playing in the Dundalk Bakers' Society. But it was likely the firm was actuated by more rational and practical considerations. My father was one of the more intelligent of the bakery operatives, a conscientious worker, well-read in his trade as well as in general scientific subjects that would have extended his knowledge to understanding of the new dough-fermenting agent.

Where before dough making had involved operations by several operatives hauling flour and water and other ingredients and laborious kneading, the new process of the doughing machine was a lone operation, needing but one operator, the dough-maker. The operation went on in the dough-loft, the floor above the bakehouse where the ovens were and the main operations of scaling and moulding took place. The dough-maker would thus have the dough-loft largely to himself, isolated from sound or sight of the work going on below. The dough was made of a ferment, called in the trade a sponge, and, of course, flour and other ingredients. The sponge had been made by other operatives several hours earlier, to allow for subsequent fermentation before dough making. After an interval for maturing, or proofing as it was called, the dough was cast through a chute on to tables in the bakehouse, where it was wrought into pieces, to be moulded and baked in the ovens.

There were intervals, maybe of a quarter to half an hour in the dough making, in which the dough-maker was free to occupy himself as he wished. In my father's case the intervals were likely to be occupied with reading. But recently he had taken to bringing in with him to the dough-loft his violin, on which he had been concentrating much practice. He had already made a repertoire of a few classical tunes and some of the better popular ballads.

It has to be explained now that next door to the bakery and divided from it by the bakery yard gate that led on to the street was John Deane's public house where from time to time the proprietor's four daughters served the customers. Alice was the senior and considered the most attractive of them, and of the bakers who had become patrons of the tavern, the dough-maker was one of her ardent suitors. The residence part of the tavern abutted onto the bakery yard, which Alice's bedroom looked on to, its window confronting the window of the bakery dough loft but twenty-feet or so opposite.

The dough-maker started work at seven in the evening and whether or not by arrangement with Alice, he had arranged his work schedule so that the interval should fall at around eleven o'clock, the time Alice customarily retired for the night. Light in her bedroom opposite became the sign for the dough-maker to take out his violin and betake himself near the dough-loft window, there to render Mendelssohn's *On Wings of Song* and other romantic melodies, his serenading usually rewarded with sight of Alice behind curtains that made at least the silhouette of her figure visible.

This was to become an almost nightly performance that started drawing an audience to the bakery yard, including some of the management personnel. It came to be heard and talked about by some of the tavern patrons, among them another of Alice's suitors, the proprietor of the butcher's shop, opposite in Church Street. Mr Joe Rogers, one of the town's rising victuallers, had a much less romantic approach in his courting. His approach was as much directed at gaining favour with Alice's father as with pressing a rather prosaic suit on Alice herself. Rogers claimed he had been notified by the Poor Law Guardians of intention to rescind contract with him for supply of sausages to the Poor House. Bread was one of the main ingredients in sausages; critics of the victualler would say, a predominant one in the composition of his sausages. He was a customer of McCann's; and he was emphatic the faults complained of in his sausages were due entirely to the sour condition of the bread, which in turn he held was to be accounted for by the frivolously faulty workmanship of the dough-maker.

I concluded the composition by adding that notwithstanding what amounted to a campaign of belittling by his rival the dough-maker's suit for Alice's favours prevailed. Perhaps it was this conclusion that won my father's approval of an essay that might have been judged, I would hold wrongly, as being an account of a somewhat irresponsible, perhaps even fatuous workman.

Some of the accounts I wrote of my father were such as could have occurred in my school days, when, for instance, I was wont to go to our sitting room, perhaps to labour on my school homework, or maybe drawn by something of social congress between my parents, and some friends. But it did not depend on the visits of friends to induce conviviality there. Here I must record that in the way of addiction to alcoholic drinks my father would be termed an occasional drinker. He could go for months without imbibing. Then, suddenly, at times without apparent prompting he would be seen to have imbibed enough to show signs of it in speech or appearance. In both these aspects normally he was fairly restrained, careful of utterance, and in his movements and dress.

When off the drink he could have qualms of conscience for his lapse, hurrying to an emporium, to pay my mother the penitence of presents, or mortification gifts. She had much tolerance, perhaps even indulgence for his lapses; though it would be uncharitable, even wrong, to think she indulged the like for profit to her trinket box or her wardrobe.

It might seem strange that what they might have termed my father's lapses into sobriety or temperance were more than tolerated by his tavern colleagues of The Temple, most of them constant and confirmed tipplers. But my father was at his best when sober, when his faculties were clear to discourse with clarity and wit, and, in the apparent distraction even to compose verse, later to be communicated in recital.

One sitting room memory I have of my father when he was in one of his lapses was his meeting with some itinerant musician or other on the street and his bringing him to our home, to be entertained by my mother. It must often have taxed her patience or tolerance. I remember one occasion when that certainly must have been the case. My father had been out with some of his tavern friends when he turned up unexpectedly accompanied by the one-man band. This versatile musician contrived to play simultaneously on accordion, a big drum and cymbals. The drum, borne on his back, took the drumbeats from drumstick tied-to and manipulated by the elbow of the musician's right arm. The cymbals were placed on top of the drum, flat, one on top of the other, with the top one tied to a cord that traversed a small pulley above, to descend behind the drum to attachment on one of the musician's heels. By motion of his leg to-and-fro the attached cord would clash the cymbals while he manipulated the accordion to give his audience a concerted as well as voluble performance.

The one-man band was a person of stature, at least in the physical sense, for apparently, encumbered as he was with his instruments, notably the big drum on his back, he could not sit down. Thus, when he entered the sitting-room, it was in an unavailed of if kindly gesture that my mother offered him a well-upholstered chair. My father introduced him with encomiums of his talents, which encouraged the musician to march to the middle of the room to start a performance. He was now directly under the gas-lit chandelier. Soon around in the room valued objects, long reposing on shelves and brackets, some remote in cupboards, started trembling in what was now a commotion of sound, and directly above the performer, where before the scintillating jets were able to say their all in the manner of refined flame, were now agitated and a-jingle.

This alarmed my mother, evidently in fear the fixture might be in danger of collapsing or falling. The chandelier was her crowning piece of furnishing. It not only added elegance to the baroque-modelled ceiling, but added a soft glow to the room's surfeit of mahogany and brass that daily polishing, under my mother's supervision, had made wan or tired-looking. In vain, with glinting, and golden-liquor-filled decanter and copious glass, did my mother try to lure the musician from the centre of the room, to continue his performance, perhaps on broad armchair or settee. Apparently he had to go through his full repertoire; and neither the sight of matured malt at hand nor the odour of fine meats coming from the kitchen was to tempt him from under the chandelier. Then my mother saw resort or recourse in noticing the piano-stool under the keyboard of the piano, the instrument, as if in deference to the night's guest musician, almost hid in a corner of the room. She eventually inveigled him to the stool, and, when awkwardly seated, he resumed his performance. But it lacked much of the former brio. For one thing, now in the sitting position he was unable to give his leg that stretch or kick to involve the cymbals atop his drum. Despite vigorous acrobatics in which his whole body was engaged, he now seemed unable to impart to his performance that rhythmic clash of sounding brass that had stirred to motion and sound the normally still and silent pendants of the chandelier.

And now my father seemed to have tired of his guest's recital, as the latter struggled to continue the performance from the piano stool. My father could easily tire of the repertoire of low-grade patriotic tunes and the repetitions of jigs and reels. This was the way with my father, often suffused with sentiment that would embrace all humanity, but with early aftermath that brought nagging hints of standards, judgements, discrimination.

Perhaps my mother planned this removal of the musician to the piano stool so my father would see it as the absurd translation or transit to the room's seat of glory, the enthronement of a talent whose more appropriate place was on the paving stones without, or the channel at the toe-path where the rain and wind swept the street's refuse to the sewers. If my father had any preference for any of the articles in the room it probably would have been for the piano and its stool. These on many occasions had served in demonstrating the musical talents of guests come to our home on social occasions. They included the town's doyen pianist, organist, violinist and vocalist, Tom Parkes.

Sometimes my father's lapses to alcohol would come at the approach of a public festival, such as Christmas or Easter. What I next wrote about him I had him at the approach of the former festival, a week or so before Christmas Eve. On this occasion he brought home with him nothing less than a quintet of real musicians, that is trained and long-practised in their profession. This was the German band, a combination of string instrumentalists who at the time were touring Ireland and Britain. They became known and much respected in the towns, where they performed as itinerants in the public highways. This was but a few years before the start of the 1914-18 War, and after the war it was said they were trained spies gathering military information for the German authorities. I first heard them on the streets in Dundalk. They discoursed the best of music, and of their pieces I can remember the waltz, I think by Ivanovici, *Waves of the Danube*.

My father had heard them performing in the main street, already showing signs of the approaching festival, and, being in festive mood himself, he invited them to our home. Surprisingly they were able to render us some of the best of the Irish melodies, but their main stock was of German music. At the intervals there was some conversation, which the hostess, my mother, seemed anxious to induce with proffered hospitality. One of the group, evidently more proficient or loquacious in English than any of his colleagues, occupied the intervals with comments on their travels in our country and comparison with the likes in Germany. Our sitting room had already been decorated for the festival with sprigs of red-berried holly and festoons of coloured bunting. The talkative musician remarked that we seemed not to have a Christmas tree and that he had not seen any either in the windows of stores or of private houses. At that time in Dundalk, and I presume in the country generally, what we now know as the Christmas tree did not appear to be popularly associated with observance of the festival. He went on to explain how popular it was in Germany and Austria. He spoke of the *Tannenbaum*, and, with the accompaniment of his violin, started to sing the popular German song of that name.

He went on to explain how in their homes in Germany the miniature, or perhaps imitation fir-tree was always a part of the domestic observances of Christmas. He described how it was dressed with baubles and other decorations, with little candles and pendant sweetmeats and nuts and wrapped gifts, especially for the children. My mother, much moved by the German's performance, and his rhapsodies about the Christmas tree, remarked what a pity it was the Christmas tree wasn't popular in Ireland. My Aunt Mary demurred, reminding my mother how that piece of holy festival observance and other symbols of pagan origin had been condemned at recent mission of the Redemptorist Fathers.

A few days before the festival a Christmas tree arrived at our home. A sturdy one, over six-feet tall, it had already been decorated with some strings of bunting. It had been delivered by one of the bakery van-men, who worked on a route towards the town of Newry. In a village on the route he had met the German band, the musicians evidently had been performing there. They had noticed the names Swift & Cooper on the van, and had arranged with the van-man to take back with him on his next delivery day a Christmas tree they were procuring for my mother.

The tree arrived the day before Christmas Eve, and, under my mother's care, it was installed in the sitting room. Already informed of the kind of decorations or accessories it should carry, it was soon laden with more bunting and glittering baubles, with little festoons of nuts and sweetmeats, small toys and miniature candles. The nuts had been left over from our Halloween party, and included two large coconuts, which were now hung near the top of the tree.

Christmas Eve brought a dull, cloud-laden afternoon; and in the sitting room perhaps the little candles and the glitter of the tinsel decorations made up a little for the partly obscured light from the chandelier, its drooping lustres now encumbered by sprigs of holly and mistletoe. It was early in the evening when my father, just parted from some of his tavern friends, and pacing homewards in Clanbrassil Street, encountered an itinerant musician new to the town. Perhaps it was the organ-grinder's selection of music, certainly unusual in a street organ, that attracted my father. The pieces were all likely of Italian origin, some of them, such as *La Donna È Mobile*, from the Verdi operas. Verdi was my father's favourite opera composer. The fact that the organ-grinder was accompanied by a monkey did not deter my father from inviting him to our home. Of course, the monkey had to come too. It was an essential accompaniment of his master and his master's performance. Perched perkily on the organ or music box, it had the business function of extending an arm towards the audience of passers-by, its hand bearing a bowl which it was hoped would become sufficiently resonant with the sound of proffered coins that it would be a kind of continuing percussion to the music.

Arrived in our sitting room, the organ-grinder and his mate were directed to a sofa at one end of the room near where the Christmas tree was standing. The musician at once placed himself at the head of the sofa, ready but waiting for signal to perform. This time the monkey did not ascend the organ, but nestled near its master on the sofa.

My Aunt Mary, probably induced by the proximity of the festival to pay one of her rare visits to the sitting room, was present, and apparently ready to forget or overlook the presence of the Christmas tree and enjoy some of the conviviality of the company. She thought to make warmer the perhaps over-formal welcome my mother had given these latest guests in our home, the organ-grinder and his mate. She made to pet the latter, fondling the creature's head and shoulders with hand strokes. Apparently encouraged by the familiarity, the creature made to disengage itself from its master, evidently to venture a leap on to my Aunt's lap, a refuge that, in my Aunt's domain the kitchen, had often given sanctuary to strayed or distraught puppies, kittens, chickens.

The organ-grinder was a tall gaunt-looking man, speaking broken English, and likely of Italian or Southern European origin. He was shabbily dressed in ill-matched tattered clothes. He seemed of the class, the deserving poor, that the local public authority, the Urban Council and the Poor Law Guardians, backed by the Church, had recommended the townsfolk should support with their charity. He was of the kind, the itinerant beggars, sometimes performers, whom my aunt succoured when they called at her kitchen door. Now noting that my father was as solicitous as herself in entertaining the organ-grinder and his companion, plying them with drinks and eatables, she remembered about his earlier recent quest, the one-man band character, also an itinerant mendicant that, but for the charity of folks on the streets, would have become a burden on the Poor Law.

My Aunt was now asking herself was my father becoming religious? Long lapsed in Church observances, he had recently, she was aware, been attending Sunday Mass, and High Mass at that, in the Cathedral. She may not have been aware that the explanation he was giving his familiars for this resumption of earlier observance was the recent changes of the music in the services in the Cathedral. Where before the organist and choir-master had worked compositions of his own, or of other mediocre music-writers not approved by the ecclesiastical authorities, into the cathedral services, the new German organist and choir-master had restored to the services the more worthy music of Mozart, Beethoven and Schubert.

Helped, no doubt, by generous quaffs of liquor, the organ-grinder was now warming to his work, and at least the Verdi pieces had a ready listener in my father who hummed in vocal accompaniment. Then a loud knock was heard on the hall-door, and after a short interval my Uncle Johnny, my father's brother, was ushered into the sitting room. He had recently retired from the police, and with his wife and some of their family was now living in a farmhouse in Rathroll, a country district about three miles south of Dundalk. He was accompanied by his dog, a taut-looking terrier, which he held on a lead. He had called, as he announced, to pay the Christmas respects. My Aunt, now the most mindful of the company regarding domestic duties or responsibilities, saw to it that my uncle and his charge were seated at as far a distance from the organ-grinder and his charge as practicable.

But my uncle was not long seated when the terrier, having observed the monkey, started growling and showing other belligerent signs. My uncle had to keep a tight rein on it to prevent its charging towards the other animal. At the same time my uncle seemed to be sharing the dog's feelings for the monkey, judging from the looks of disgust with which the uncle was now regarding my father's perhaps mawkish fondling of the animal. Probably the uncle was bringing to mind earlier debates with my father, a firm believer in the evolution of species, and how he, his brother, refuted and scorned Darwin's theory of our simian origin.

As the evening proceeded and the glasses kept clinking it was noticed the music was being subjected to sudden stops and changes of tempo, due, no doubt, to the irregular manipulation of his instrument by the organ-grinder. Perhaps the monkey had sensed that the lead restraining its movements was no longer in the controlling hand of its master, when it gave a sudden leap from the organ to land near the foot of the Christmas tree. It was but seconds when it was near the top of the tree and making its choice of the little bundles of eatables hung on the twigs.

The creature's leap on to the tree was the signal for Uncle Johnny's dog, perhaps not unaided, to bound forward towards the tree, to start a commotion of yelping and snarling. Whether in search of safer refuge, the monkey started exploring the higher reaches of the tree from which some of the heavier articles displayed were suspended. Then one of the big coconuts seemed to have got released for it fell floor-wards to crash on the yelping terrier's head.

There were a few seconds silence, followed by an agonised cry from the terrier, to be quickly responded to by its owner, now scrambling in haste to the rescue. When the animal was quietened a bit, he found it bleeding from the snout, much, I suppose, as a human would bleed from a punch on the nose. And as humans, notably boxers, usually recover none the worse from the like, uncle Johnny's dog was likely to live to fight another day, but perhaps not under a Christmas tree. For the Uncle Johnny, he had come to tender good wishes for the festival. It was hardly Happy Returns that he had to return to Rathroll with a wounded terrier, one that had served him so well, hunting rabbits and hares. He went home with the sympathy of my aunt likely to be strongest in his mind. She commented that the Redemptorists were right. The tree was bringing bad luck to the place.

I concluded the composition with note that my father was sorry for the Uncle Johnny on account of the accident to the dog, and recommended I should next write an essay on his brother. I thought about the latter of a few years back when, before his retirement from the police force, the Royal Irish Constabulary, he sometimes came to our home to spend part of his annual holidays. He was then stationed in some small town in County Carlow.

My uncle had, at least then the six feet of height the police authorities would like all recruits to have mustered before presenting themselves for entry in the force. He had what most would have regarded as a handsome face, gracefully curved in the cheeks and nose. This roundness of features also to a noticeable extent marked the contours of his shoulders, so that the neck above seemed a bit elongated and the chest below a bit embarreled. Altogether these features of his appearance would hardly be regarded as the model of one charged with the duties of law-enforcement. By contrast, my father, a few inches short of his brother in height, had more the angular cast of features which, with straight broad shoulders that protruded the chest, could give one the impression of the firmness and dignity conceived as being associated with law-enforcement. But, of course, my parent had not at all the temperament for such. I am sure that all the laws my father would have liked to have enforced would be concerned with the regulation of affairs in the socialist utopias he was disposed to conjure when debating politics with his friends. Apart from that, his interest in law-enforcement might have relevance in the literary domain. Himself a good verse-writer, he might have affirmed that poetasters, of whom there was current a plethora of bores, might be obliged to conform with standards of clarity, wit and grace, as exemplified in Byron and Burns, with Thomas Moore my father's favourite poets.

What my uncle lacked in the appearance of being a stern law-enforcer he tried to make up in his manner or habit of talking about the law, often with people who would have no knowledge of or interest in the laws concerned. The habit was much to be observed when he came to our home. When he came on visits he kept mostly to our kitchen where he had as listeners my Aunt Mary, her husband, John Cooper, if not at work, and the domestic help. My aunt and her husband were the most law-abiding of persons. As for the domestic-help, or servant, as she was usually called, she was too young, probably too unadventuresome, to ponder much on all the possibilities of law breaking that might confront her. In his homilies on the law my uncle was in the habit of pacing to and fro in the kitchen, the sound of his stoutly-soled boots on the flagged floor giving the impression he was on the beat.

This time the uncle, then stationed in County Carlow, had come to our home to spend a week or so of his annual leave. As on the few previous similar occasions he had made the kitchen his headquarters, alternating his pacing the floor and tending his sporting gun and his fishing rod, with associated accessories. For several days he had been out fishing on the Castletown River, a moderately sized waterway that skirted the Southern end of the town. It offered fairly worthwhile fishing for trout, with an occasional chance of a salmon. For four or five of the days he had been out on the riverbank he had caught nothing. Then, coming near the end of his holiday, he returned with a large salmon.

There were congratulations and something like general rejoicing in the kitchen that evening as we sat at the table to enjoy the salmon meal. For the sake of family sociability on the occasion of the uncle's stay, my parents, normally disposed to take their meals in the sitting room, came to eat and sup in the kitchen. Apart from the fact that the uncle felt more at home in the kitchen, there were the instances of his dining with my parents in the sitting room when unpleasant, sometimes bitter discussion on political matters arose between my father and his brother. My father was a republican nationalist with socialist leaning, whilst his brother, as was to be expected of members of the Royal Irish Constabulary, felt political loyalty to the British Crown.

As the salmon was a very large one only half of it was used for this family meal in the kitchen. By direction of my aunt the remaining portion was deposited in the meat-safe, a wire-meshed box that hung on the wall outside near the kitchen door. It was arranged it would provide a further salmon meal the following evening. On that afternoon, in preparing for the meal, the aunt sent the servant to fetch the half salmon from the meat-safe. The servant returned to the kitchen to report the half-salmon wasn't there and the meat-safe was empty.

It was late that afternoon when the Uncle Johnny entered the kitchen, his fishing rod and canvas bag disclosing he had been out again on the riverbank. As on the early days of his vacation, in divesting himself of the empty bag he had to report that fishing was bad on the river that day. My aunt was busy preparing for the evening meal. When she thought he had noticed the preparations were for a meal other than that of the half-salmon left from the previous evening she nervously told him what had happened. She explained how Julia had gone to the meat-safe out in the yard, and how she found the safe empty, the half-fish gone. As if challenged to duty, the uncle ordered the domestic before him. He started the interrogation evidently determined to unearth the facts of a piece of blaguardism or crime that had purloined the piece of property he had committed to the care of his brother's household.

Julia at first responded with the simple account of going out to the meat-safe, opening the safe and finding it empty. She then reported looking around in the vicinity of the meat-safe, with the idea of a cat or perhaps some strange bird had invaded the safe. Julia made this latter suggestion with ill-repressed tittering, a development her interrogator could not but have regarded as contempt for the law. He then practically accused her of having stolen the piece of fish.

This brought Julia to a more serious mien. Herself becoming accuser, and addressing her remarks more to my aunt, she alleged my uncle had not caught that salmon, but had bought it from her uncle. Her uncle, Tim Madden, was an angler well known among his kindred in the district, and who lately was being suspected by the local police of being a poacher. This halted the interrogation, and the seemingly outraged uncle, whether from astonishment or embarrassment, lapsed into a mood showing something of incredulousness.

Later he made random remarks to my aunt, and her spouse, now arrived in the kitchen from work in the bakery. The remarks, somewhat vague and made in a desultory way, seemed to be to the effect that when he, the uncle, had hooked the salmon and was having difficulty in landing it, another angler on the bank near him, a stranger he did not know, helped him with a hand-net to land the unusually large fish.

By the time the household sat down to the alternative or substitute meal of steak and onions, which my aunt and her help prepared, there was silence about the matter. All at the table were mute, but evidently a bit on edge or expectant, the Uncle Johnny obviously restless, his lower limbs trying to come to terms with the chair he kept trying to steady, limbs that might have felt more comfortable on the beat. There he was, the Uncle Johnny, Constable John Laurence Swift, looking more the accused than in his normal professional role of accuser, now attired in dark-grey home-spun-looking clothes, bespeaking the married constabulary-man's domestic ménage that did its own boot-and-shoe-repairing and its own hair-cutting, in a domestic economy obliged not to be beholden to many in a community in which few were friendly, fewer trustful.

With all in the house, including the domestic help, seated at the meal, there was what would be called ominous silence till towards the end my mother, perhaps undiplomatically, complimented my aunt on the excellent meal she had prepared as alternative to the missing one. This, of course, had the effect of a challenge to the Uncle Johnny. He steadied himself, and in laboured fashion went on to explain how on the day in question he, out fishing, had hooked this unusually large salmon, that was tugging so strongly on his fishing line, he had to steady himself on the river bank, lest he be pulled into the river. Another angler, a perfect stranger to him, on the bank nearby, had observed his difficulties in landing the fish and had offered to help with his hand-net. Net in hand this stranger waded out towards the centre of the river and netted the fish. In coming back to the bank the heel of one of the man's long-legged fishing boots got caught in boulders at the river-edge, with the result the heel was wrenched off the boot. The Uncle Johnny went on to explain that for the service this stranger had rendered him in landing that salmon he felt obliged to compensate the man for the loss of the heel from his boot. So he gave the man ten shillings.

This seemed the fullest explanation yet of the incident; and if the uncle, in concluding his account, was looking round the table at the reaction of his hearers, he would see eyes and eyebrows raised in surprise or incredulousness. That is, all but in the case of my father. He showed signs of not only giving credence to, but of being nothing less than elated by his brother's account. Was this just charitableness on my father's part, offered perhaps for some verbal trouncing he had recently given the brother on some political or other questions on which they radically differed? Or was my father's credence accorded not just to an example of the literal or factual truth but rather to what my father would call truth of the imagination and which he sometimes termed poetic truth, the element which he held was in all great works of literature and art?

Chapter 10

It was 1924 when, feeling fit enough to work at the normal commercial bakery trade as I knew it in Dublin, my membership of the union was restored, and I was admitted to work off the slate, that is the casual list from which extra hands or replacements were sent to the different bakeries as required. In the few years interval of my absence union organisation had been extended in Dublin and other parts of the country. The firm in which I had been earlier employed and from which I had been dismissed for trying to recruit for the union, Messrs Bewley's, was now a union house.

By a strange turn this was the bakery to which I was sent when only but a few mornings reporting on the slate. I was temporarily to replace a permanent worker on sick leave. I was but a few days working there when the head of the firm, Mr Ernest Bewley, sent for me to attend at his office. He informed me he had heard of my conscription experience in England during the War, of how I had been imprisoned with some of his British co-religionists, Quakers, in resisting compulsory military service in the War. He offered me a permanent job in the bakery. I was glad to accept, for I was already to some extent familiar with the general run of work in the bakery. Besides, I thought it would be getting some of my own back, so to speak, on the foreman, Fred Andrews, still in charge, who had eight years before sacked me for recruiting for the union. Some years later I was to replace him as the bakery foreman.

Early on in this second term with the Bewley firm I was elected by the bakery staff to represent them on the union's management committee. There were now ample facilities from the firm for union representative to exercise union duties. In this way I became more and more involved in union activities extending beyond the confines of the firm. On the union's committee of management I was elected Chairman of the Union's Disputes' Committee. This body had to do with the running of trade disputes in which the union was involved. Although the union was now generally well organised in Dublin, there were some small bakeries and some new ones starting which were resisting union organisation. The Disputes' Committee had much success in action against these firms, and soon it became rare to find a bakery in the city whose workers were not organised in the union.

Parallel with the Disputes Committee, or perhaps rather as an offshoot of it, we organised the Bakery Trade's Social Club. It was started to cater for the social interests or activities of the union members and their families. I was made chairman of the committee. At first our activities were recreational, the organising of football and billiard competitions among members and the running of weekly dances for members and their friends. The activities were partly financed by weekly ballot draws, for which tickets were circulated to union members in all the Dublin bakeries. This was well supported by the members and their friends, as were also the weekly dances. Later the football competitions were extended to embrace union teams in the provinces, embracing teams in Belfast, Limerick and Waterford as well as Dublin.

With revenue now coming from the weekly ballots and the dances, we started more serious activities. We took on to cater for some of the cultural interests of the members of the union and their friends. We started a choir and orchestra. Among the members of the union in Dublin at the time there were some instrumentalists who had played in city bands, in some cases ex-members of the British Army, former military bandsmen. Along with these there were children of union members enrolled in music classes in the city. From these we started an orchestra of wind and stringed instruments. We started with around twenty members in the group. We made provision for the group to be added to by financing the enrolment of members' children in the Dublin College of Music, then known as the Municipal School of Music. The Principal of the School at the time was Arthur Darley, a celebrity violinist in his day, whose son, also Arthur, was later to become Medical Officer of the union.

The orchestra was under the tutorship of a Mr May, one of a well-known musical family of that name. The choir was trained by a Mr Power, who was a singing teacher and lead singer in one of the leading church choirs in the city. His place as our choir-master was later taken by Leo Maguire, long actively associated with the Dublin Grande Opera Society and well-known from musical broadcasting activities. Both the choir and orchestra gave public concerts in the Father Matthew Hall and in the Rathmines Town Hall. They were able to perform creditably standard concert works of classical composers such as Beethoven and Schubert as well as works by our own Wallace and Balfe, and, of course, Moore's Melodies figured prominently in their programmes. Both the orchestra and choir went on performing for a few years. The orchestra was the first to disintegrate, I believe principally by the development of popular dancing in the Thirties and the proliferation of small commercial dance-bands. The choir lasted to perform at union functions, down to its last performance when, in combination with the choir and brass-and-reed band of the Irish Transport and General Workers' Union it performed at the opening of the International Union of Food and Allied Workers' Associations' Congress held in Liberty Hall, Dublin in 1967.

Another promotion of the Bakery Trade's Social Committee's extended activities was the Dublin Bakery School. This was started in 1935 in the premises of the Union's Headquarters, 37 Lower Gardiner Street. We influenced the Union's Management Committee to make a grant to equip a small bakery in a mews at the back of the premises. As the bakery trade in Ireland had no traditions or native sources of bakery trade education, we were obliged to look to the trade in Britain for a qualified teacher. We were lucky enough to get a graduate from the Birmingham Bakery School, Sam Anthony, a qualified bakery school teacher, a Welshman, who was glad to come to Dublin to be associated with an educational project that had been conceived by a trade union.

I suppose we had material as well as cultural or idealistic motives in promoting such projects as a choir, an orchestra and a bakery trade school. At the time, the Thirties, culture was largely regarded as something of class privilege. The opera that came seasonally to the Gaiety Theatre, or the odd celebrity concert, at the Theatre Royal or the Capitol, were generally regarded as entertainment for the upper and middle classes. Starting cultural activities in a trade union could be regarded as a challenge to that, an assertion that the working-class had full rights to the broadest cultural life, and in economic terms should have the wherewithal to avail of such a life. Trade Union demands should not be limited to the mere bread-and-butter essential to living.

The same material interest could be associated with our promotion of the bakery school. The Union's claims for higher wages and better working conditions for its members could be made much stronger when made on behalf of workers who were educated, and educated by their own efforts, at their trade. My father had died in 1926, following protracted illness from paralysis. Perhaps it was his death and my knowledge of the leading role he had earlier played as a trade union activist that influenced me, at least in part, when the following year, 1927, I took on active duties in my union as Chairman of its Disputes Committee and Social Committee. This, of course, was part-time or spare-time work, for I was still working at the trade in Messrs Bewley's, part of the time, for a few years, in fact, as a bakery foreman. The two sons, Victor and Alfred, of the deceased Ernest Bewley were now at the head of the Bewley management, and it said much for the management's liberal attitude that I was able whilst holding responsibilities in the bakery to devote much of my time to union affairs. Alfred Bewley served part of his apprenticeship under me at that time. Later under the brothers' management the progressive attitude was further developed when changes in management structure brought workers' elected representatives on to the board. Perhaps these changes were hastily conceived or ill-structured, but some years later the firm came up against financial problems which have brought about change in ownership and management of more orthodox business outlook.

In 1936 I became a whole-time official of the union. On August 27th 1936 the day after my fortieth birthday I was elected National Organiser at the Union's National Delegate Conference. This position gave me more time to devote to some of the educational and cultural activities in which I was already involved in the Social Committee. Soon after the Bakery School was established in the union premises in Gardiner Street, Dublin its work, displayed at the Royal Dublin Society's Spring Show in 1936, came under the notice of the City of Dublin Vocational Education Authorities. As a result it was agreed with the union that the Bakery School should come under the administration of the authorities, subject to the union's exercising control as to the nomination of students to the school courses. The nomination of apprentices to the bakery trade in Dublin had for many years been a function of the trade union, with the agreement of the bakery employers, which only in rare cases was withheld. This arrangement was continued when the City of Dublin Vocational Education Committee took over the running of the School in 1937. The School then came under a Supervisory Committee made up of representatives of the union and of the Dublin Master Bakers' Committee. I was Chairman of that Committee up to the year of my retirement from the General Secretaryship of the Union in 1967. Under the Supervisory Committee's regulations it was made compulsory for apprentices to attend the school and pass the examinations through the four years of apprenticeship.

Shortly after the founding of the Dublin Bakery School the Belfast Bakery School started, again from the initiative of the union. Later bakery education classes were started in Limerick and Drogheda. This development of education in the trade enabled the Social Committee to extend its activities to promoting bakery trade exhibitions, another means of advancing standards in the trade, the standards in mind being those of quality of ingredients, quality of workmanship and hygiene. The first exhibition was held in the union premises in Gardiner Street in 1938. The work of members in the union's main branches, including the North, was submitted in competitions for prizes and certificates. The competitions covered the main classes of bakery both in bread and confectionery.

The following year, 1939, a larger exhibition was held in the Engineers' Hall, Dawson Street, Dublin. This was formally opened by the then Minister for Industry and Commerce, Mr Seán Lemass.

Due again to the work of the Social Committee, the union at its Delegate Conference in 1938 decided to affiliate to the International Union of Food, Drink and Tobacco Workers. During the War (1939-45) it was not practicable for the union to run trade exhibitions. But, the war over, through the initiative of the Social Committee, exhibition promotion was restarted when, with the co-operation of the International Union, a series of three international bakery trade exhibitions was held in Dublin. This brought into exhibition and competition samples of bakery products from several countries in Europe, including the Soviet Union, and from the U.S.A. The third of these exhibitions, all held in the Mansion House, Dublin, took place in 1953, when an added feature at the exhibition was the running of the international apprentices' working competitions, when teams of bakery apprentices from England, Scotland and our own country showed their skill at the trade in the exhibition premises. This feature was arranged by the joint committee representative of the English and Scottish and our own Bakery Workers' Unions.

This change of work since 1936, from the largely manual operations in the bakery to the more sedentary duties of the full-time union official altered the trend of my labour history, my work now being largely of the office kind, with visits to the union's branches and attendances at conferences. I was now missing the physical exercise of work in the bakery. I tried to make up for this with long walks and other forms of physical exercise which I contrived to practice in the evenings. My visits to the branches were made by train or bus. I preferred the train, as both reading and writing were possible on train journeys. The union executive wanted to provide me with a car, but I informed them I could not drive a motor car and was not desirous of learning to drive. When I visited the branches I tried to put in walks prior to the branch meetings usually held at night.

When the Social Committee had got going with its many activities, in sport and recreation, and later the choir and orchestra and the Bakery School, we began to feel the need for suitable premises. In the Twenties and into the Thirties there was much agitation, particularly in the Labour Party, for what was called proper housing for the workers and doing away with the slum dwellings. In the Thirties new housing schemes had been developed in areas not far from the city's centre, new suburbs that were a great improvement on the tenement slums formerly housing working-class families. We used this change as an argument that the Union's Headquarters, then in Gardiner Street, in a slum tenement area, should be accommodated in premises more in keeping with the housing changes now taking place.

The Social Committee now had influence on the Union's National Executive, and was able to have a motion adopted at the 1943 National Delegate Meeting authorising the Executive to take measures to procure new premises capable of catering for the social and cultural interests of the members.

I was elected General Secretary of the Union in 1943, and was given the task by the Executive of looking out for suitable premises or sites to meet the resolution passed by the Delegate Conference. After some considerable searching in the city, premises in Harcourt Street, a prestigious thoroughfare not far from the city centre, were viewed and, with alterations, thought suitable. It was the old Baptist Church, opposite the railway station, and from a declining congregation, was now on the market for sale. The church had an old gothic front elevation in granite, extending along seventy-feet in Harcourt Street. The service part of the church, with caretaker's house and yard, went back farther than that to Charlotte Street, that linked up with Camden Street. The union paid ten thousand pounds for the property, subject to an annual ground rent to the Hely-Hutchinson Estate, of around twenty pounds.

We engaged Michael Scott, then one of the foremost city architects to transform the building to our requirements of providing not only the necessary union administration quarters, but also facilities for catering for the social and cultural interests of the union's members and their friends. The foundation stone for the re-structured premises was laid by Alderman Martin O'Sullivan, Lord Mayor of Dublin, the first Labour Lord Mayor of the City. When the alterations were made and the building suitably furnished, the formal opening, by the then Minister for Industry and Commerce, Mr Seán Lemass, took place in February 1946. There was somewhat of an embarrassment at the formal opening. The executive had arranged a dinner in the main auditorium of the building. Cultural bodies, including the two Dublin Universities, the Royal Irish Academy and the Metropolitan School of Art were invited to send representatives to the function. Representatives of these bodies attended. It was also decided to invite the Roman Catholic Archbishop of Dublin, Dr. John Charles McQuaid and the Church of Ireland Archbishop of Dublin, Dr. Barton, to the function. The latter accepted and attended. But Dr. McQuaid did not, intimating that as the function was being held during Lent he could not attend.

In the interim between acquiring the Baptist Church and the altered premises being made ready for the formal opening I got authority from the executive to start collecting books for a suitable lending library to be housed in the premises. With some help from Paddy Stephenson, then assistant librarian in Kevin Street Public Library, and later Chief City Librarian, I started collecting books thought suitable for inclusion in a trade union library. Paddy Stephenson was greatly in sympathy with this as a trade union undertaking. A member of the Fianna that served under Connolly in the General Post Office in Easter Week, 1916, Paddy Stephenson had strong socialist sympathies. In the selection of books I was also helped by John Quinn, head of the second-hand book department of Messrs Eason's. He too was sympathetic with the idea of a trade union library particularly in sociological works. He had a great knowledge of books, particularly of the commercial value of second-hand works. In his work in Eason's he often had to assess the value of and acquire whole libraries of books on the market.

Before I began collecting books suitable for the library there had to be some guiding principles agreed as to their choice. At the time vigilance bodies were operating watching libraries and the books they were circulating. I got the union executive to agree, first of all, that, as it was to be a trade union library, works in the social sciences should predominate in it. This would embrace established works in economics, sociology and labour history. The library should also contain recognised works in literature and the arts, particularly of Irish authors. There should also be available books on the bakery and associated trades, particularly of the technical kind that could be helpful to bakery school students. Within such general range it was agreed that the books to be available in the union's library could be such as might be found in the city's public libraries, and thus coming under the imprimatur of the City Public Libraries' Committee.

The library was formally opened in 1947 by the then Lord Mayor of Dublin, John McCann, T.D., himself an Abbey Theatre dramatist. The book collection then numbered around eight thousand volumes. Works in the social sciences embraced those of Connolly, Marx, Engels, Lenin, as well as the standard works of Adam Smith, Jevons, John Stuart Mill, Marshall, Tolstoy and others. The drama section contained the works of Shaw, Wilde and O'Casey, as well as of the better-known British authors, including Shakespeare. Prominent in the poetry section were the works of Thomas Moore, Goldsmith and Robert Burns.

There were several pieces of sculpture in wood panels in appropriate parts of the library. These included, in the centre panel, a full bust of James Connolly, cast in tunic of the Citizen Army, and described as Bakery Worker, Trade Union Leader, Teacher, Soldier. The other panels had, in appropriate places, profiles of Goldsmith, Moore, Yeats, Shaw and O'Casey. These pieces of sculpture were executed by Hilary Heron, a relative of Archie Heron, then prominent in the Labour Party, who was married to one of Connolly's daughters.

The library was on the first-floor of the building. During the day it served also as a restaurant, and at night also catered for social parties. It became a popular place for wedding breakfasts.

On the floor above the library was what was known as the Guild Room. This was used for lectures and film shows. It was equipped with two film-projectors. There were regular shows for the children's film club, constituted of children of union members. It was also used for ballet classes for the children. Others to use the Guild Room for regular practise were the Dublin Orchestral Players, under the directorship of Brian Boydell.

The main auditorium on the ground-floor was used for meetings and conferences. For such it had been used by the Irish Trade Union Congress and the Labour Party as well as by the union itself and other organisations.

It was also used for nightly dances, and for these the permanent house band, the Four Provinces Orchestra, performed. The combination was called after the name given the premises. Four Provinces House, signifying that the union had members in all four provinces of the country. The leader of the band, Ted Johnson, was a member of the union, who once worked at the trade, but was now a professional musician. He was one of the founding members of our earlier orchestra. Another member of the house band was Paddy Malone, pianist, and for some time General Secretary of the Musicians' Federation. Another fully professional member was Johnny Devlin. He, as well as playing in the group, did the arrangements of music, including programmes for special performances. These would include arrangements for playing national anthems when foreign delegates would be attending union functions. Johnny Devlin later took up a leading appointment in the Radio Éireann Light Orchestra.

The walls of this main hall of Four Provinces House were decorated with murals. One section of the murals was executed by leading artist at the time, Frances Kelly. She was the wife of Dr. Fredrick Boland, a distinguished official of the Department of External Affairs, who at one time served as President of the United Nations Organisation. Their daughter, Evan Boland, has become prominent as a poet. The subjects of Frances Kelly's murals, on the story of bread-making in Dublin, were taken from my soon to be published book, *History of the Dublin Bakers and Others*. A colleague artist, Nano Reid, executed the other group of murals on the auditorium's walls. These had Irish Labour significance, one depicting Larkin addressing a meeting in College Green, Dublin, another showing Connolly at a meeting on Belfast Docks. Yet another was devoted to the Ralahine Co-operative, whilst one featured Irish Labour writing, with O'Casey as the main person portrayed.

Another artist engaged for the embellishment of the building was Laurence Campbell, sculptor. He had carved and gilded stone panels that appeared at the main entrance to the building. The panels depicted aspects of the bakery trade and the historic background of the Labour Movement. Of the latter one panel depicted workers being whipped through the Coombe for transgressing the Combination laws. Another panel showed similar delinquents being put aboard ship for transportation to a penal colony.

Four Provinces House was going just over two years when rumours started circulating that were seriously to affect its activities and business. The rumours were to the effect that the place was something like a centre for communism. Communist meetings were alleged to be held there and there were communist books in the library. Some of the rumours were directed at myself. In the previous decade I had come under criticism in the more virulent of the Catholic press. In 1933 I had been associated with the founding of the Secular Society of Ireland. The main object of the Society was to free education from control by the churches. I was chairman of the Society, Owen Sheehy

Skeffington was vice-chairman, and Niall O'Leary-Curtis, a civil servant, was secretary. Captain Jack White, the trainer of the Citizen Army, was an active member. Some prominent literary people were members. They included Denis Johnston, the playwright, and the critic, Mary Manning.

We found it hard to get a place for meetings, but found temporary shelter in the rooms of the Contemporary Club, at the time a more or less private debating society that used to meet on Saturday nights in Lincoln Chambers, at the back of Trinity College. At one of the Secular Society's meetings it happened a reporter of the *Irish Press* was present, and next morning in that periodical appeared what would be regarded as an exposure of our Society and its aims. The Catholic periodicals took up the report, and soon there were strident warnings about the new Godless organisation.

This had the intimidating effect intended, and soon the membership of the Society started to dwindle. We could now find no place that we could rent to hold a meeting, and we had to resort to ad-hoc meetings in one-another's homes. This went on in desultory fashion until 1936, by which time, in the fine weather, we were reduced to meeting in the open air, such as in strolls or picnics in the Dublin Mountains. At the last such al fresco meeting held that year, when we were reduced to around half a dozen active members, we decided to disband the Society, and perhaps come together again when prospects might be more promising. Franco's rebellion against the Spanish Republican Government had just begun, and we decided to send the Society's funds we had in hands to aid the Spanish Government. We had found that, though few people wanted to be actively associated with the Society by attending meetings or otherwise showing themselves zealous, they were quite willing to support it financially.

Some of us then helped in forming the Spanish Aid Committee. This body was active during the Spanish Civil War, helping practically in whatever way it could, including support of the International Brigade, and in publicity in efforts to expose the fascist character of the Franco and Salazar campaigns. Mrs Hanna Sheehy Skeffington, Owen's mother, was Chairwoman of the Spanish Aid Committee, I was Vice-Chairman, and Miss Bobby Walshe was Treasurer. With the help of some active members of my union, I was able to organise among members in the Dublin bakeries weekly collection for the Spanish Aid Fund.

At the same time during these decades of the Thirties there was little response from the Irish trade unions generally to the dangers of Fascism's rise in Europe. The apparent support of Fascism by the Roman Catholic Church appeared the main cause of this, even trade union leaders, formerly vocal, even vociferous, in advocating socialist principles, choosing now to be silent or timorous in face of the fascist threat.

If a date could be meaningfully put to the start of the events here under review it could be 1929, the date of the Latern Treaty between Pope Pius XI and Mussolini 's fascist government. This created the present Vatican City State, along with affecting other changes in the relations between the Vatican and Mussolini 's government. Two years later, in 1931, the same Pontiff issued his encyclical, *Quadragessimo Anno*. It commemorated the fortieth anniversary of the *Rerum Novarum* encyclical issued by Pope Leo XIII. Both encyclicals were anti-socialist in their texts, and advocated the setting up of vocational organisations, embracing jointly employers and workers on the lines of the medieval guilds. The doctrine became known as Corporatism, and in practice was to be seen in the fascist regimes, first, from the early Twenties in Italy, then in the early Thirties in Hitler's Germany and Salazar's Portugal. Franco's fascist state came towards the end of the Thirties. In all these cases where corporatism had come to power the trade unions and other democratic organisations were suppressed and often their leaders imprisoned or liquidated.

I have reason to believe that my association with the Secular Society and the Spanish Aid Committee, along with my generally known hostility to fascism, were in the mind of those promoting the campaign against our library. Towards the end of 1948 the boycott of the premises by the many bodies that had been routinely using it showed how effective the campaign was. These regularly booking groups for dances and other social functions included medical students' and nurses' organisations and sports clubs. Over the two years since the opening of the premises the revenue from these lettings and from other earnings in the premises had netted the union a profit of around twenty thousand pounds, which recouped much of the union's funds spent on the project.

The union executive decided to get rid of the library, disposing of the eight thousand books to Messrs Greene book-sellers, for six hundred pounds. The executive then sought tenants for the parts of the premises in which the social functions were run. The tenancy was taken up by what became known as Lorcan Bourke Enterprises. Lorcan Bourke was a well-known theatre impresario in the city. One of his daughters married Eamonn Andrews, who became associated with the tenancy. By that time Eamonn Andrews had become a luminary in the British Broadcasting Corporation. Another theatre impresario, Fred O'Donovan, was on the tenancy board. He later became chairman of the R.T.E. Authority.

Possibly under the influence of Eamonn Andrews, the tenancy changed its name to the Television Club. It apparently did good business for several years; but perhaps from rumoured differences on the board and maybe a decline in the kind of entertainment for which the board was catering, the tenancy came to an end. This, presumably, influenced the union executive to sell the premises, which they duly did to a property developer in the 1980s.

When in 1936 I became a full-time trade union official it brought many changes not only in my labour but in my general mode of life. I was to widen my union interest in extended fields of union activities. I became a delegate to the Dublin Trades Union Council in 1933. From 1943 to '45 I was Vice-President of the Council, with Jim Larkin, Senior, as President. I became President of the Council in 1945, relinquishing the position later that year to become Vice-President of the Irish Trade Union Congress. I became President of that body in 1946, and later was the Congress Treasurer for eight years. Also in 1946 I was elected to Management Committee of the International Union of Food and Allied Workers' Associations. In 1955 I became Vice-President, and in 1964 President of that body. Over this period with the International Union I did much travel in Europe and in the U.S.A. in connection with union activities. Such were some of the changes consequent in my becoming a full-time union official in 1936.

It brought another change, which was to have significance in the writing of this narrative or account. When I took up the full-time position in 1936 my main duties as National Organiser was to visit the union's branches and to explore the possibilities of starting new branches. One of my early visits was to the Dundalk branch. There were special reasons for this, of course, Dundalk being my native town, and the branch having had at one time my father as its President.

This local branch of our national union still liked to preserve its old title of the Dundalk Bakers' Society. It was a young man, Owen Hanratty, who was now the branch secretary. He would have been regarded by the branch as somewhat of a scholar, as he had gone through most of the classes in the local school of the Irish Christian Brothers. Owing to the early death of his father, who had been a baker, Ownie had been obliged to become a bread-winner before completing his schooling, to help support the widowed mother and a few younger children. It was his considerable schooling that influenced the members in making him branch secretary shortly after he completed his apprenticeship. Ownie wasn't happy working at the baking trade. He was not of strong physique and was subject to chest trouble. He nursed ambitions of becoming a writer of some kind, perhaps, for a start, a correspondent or reporter for a newspaper. It had been noted his writing of the minutes of the Society's transactions had been developing something of a literary flavour about them.

I was drawn much to Ownie Hanratty from the first time I met him, that is shortly after I was appointed National Organiser of the Union. He was a nephew of the yardman who had worked in our bakery, Pat Quigley, who like most, if not all, who had worked for us, was now dead some considerable time. As his uncle had been, Hanratty was a resident of Toberona, but in the latter's case the dwelling was of the modern artisan kind that were now appearing in rural areas as part of urban extension.

So I now found myself, after a number of years, visiting Toberona again. Hanratty and his young wife made me welcome, she being almost as avid as he to hear me talk about the old days when I used to visit the Quigley cottage with my father. Ownie was particularly curious to know about the doings of his uncle. But when this subject was exhausted he wanted to know much about my father's history, from the time he was an officer of the Dundalk Bakers' Society to when he was running the bakery in Clanbrassil Street. He also wanted to be informed about my father's and his uncle's associates, particularly about the habitués of Conlon's tavern, The Temple.

These subjects did not exhaust Owen Hanratty 's curiosity, for in the several visits I paid his home he showed interest in my own history. He had come to taking notes on what I was narrating, and this came to cover practically everything of note in which I was involved from my school days to my becoming a full-time trade union official. When I realised Ownie Hanratty was taking notes of what were becoming my reminiscences I remembered my father's account of the Templars' admonition or warning to those would bore them with tedious accounts: Tell it in Toberona

There was much more to my experiences as a union official than I was able to narrate to Hanratty. He died in the early forties. By that time, 1943, I had become General Secretary of my own union and later a member of the Management Committee of the International Union of Food and Allied Workers' Associations. I was to have twenty-one years tenure on the International Union's governing body, becoming President in 1964. My retiring from that position in 1967 and, at the same time, my giving up my position as General Secretary of my own union, ended my active life in the union movement. At the time of my retiring from these positions I had been forty years in what may be called corporate membership, that in participating on union committees, executives and councils. I had started this in 1927, when I became chairman of sub-committees in my own union.

When I retired from the General Secretaryship of my union forty years later I was not obliged to go out. There was not in the union's rules any age limit determining when the official should retire. I was approaching seventy-one years of age when I retired, and I was in sufficiently good health to be able to carry out the duties for some time in the future. I felt the Union Executive and the members generally had the same view of it. The fact was I had become somewhat frustrated in the work I was doing. When, in 1927, I became an active committee member in my branch of the union the urge I felt must have been something like what earnest church initiates describe as the call of vocation. I saw the work of endeavouring to raise the living standards and improve the working conditions of the workers with whom I worked as a worthy pursuit. That the living standard aimed at should embrace cultural values gave zest to the work. But after some years of trying to promote cultural activities in the union I was made realise that the leaders generally of the movement had not much sympathy with such aim.

The trade unions had settled down to what was called collective bargaining, haggling over wage-rates and working conditions. I had conceived trade unionism as having a broader base or broader potentials than that. In 1938 I paid my first visit to the Soviet Union, and my experiences there confirmed my view that trade unions had potentialities beyond the function of collective bargaining. Subsequent visits to the Soviet Union confirmed me in this. I had seen something of the manifold economic and social functions in which the Soviet trade unions were active, how they participated in the state planning organs, in the management of work places, in the administration of the social services and the promotion of cultural activities.

In my retirement from active trade union work I still felt I should try to do something in promoting this broader conception of the trade union. I had been a member of the Irish Labour Party since 1927. I was a member mainly because my trade union was affiliated to the Party, and from the conviction that the broader objectives I saw for the trade unions were political and were to be attained by political action. From that time to the time I had been active in the Party and had served for a few years on its Administrative Council, I found the Labour Party leadership too given to pandering to rural constituency politics, too timorous of offending church directives or admonitions on political questions.

In 1968, a year after my retirement from the General Secretaryship of my union I became active in a Labour Party group that was campaigning for the assertion of clearer socialist policies by the Party. I had drafted a policy statement on industrial democracy, which was adopted by the 1969 delegate conference. It contained proposals for workers' participation in the management of work places generally. It was edited and given the title of *Workers' Democracy* by the Party's General Secretary at the time, Brendan Halligan.

Being of the belief that democracy is to be assessed by the extent to which people participate in decision-making, it seems to me a curtailment of the right to democracy to exclude workers from decision-making in the work-place. I believe the greatest contribution that what we call the Russian Revolution of 1917 has been the democratisation of the economic processes, from planning the uses to be made of resources to their utilisation.

In 1966, the year before my retirement from active trade union work, I took part in establishing the Ireland-U.S.S.R. Friendship Society. Other founders of the Society at the time were Frank Edwards and his wife, Bobby Edwards (née Walshe) and Brendan Scott, the three since deceased. Among surviving founders were Nora Harkin, Angela McQuillan and George Lawlor.

I have not taken to a withdrawn or sedentary retirement. I can take to long stretches of writing and reading at home, but I am subject to spells of impatience to be out meeting people and being involved outside domestic calls. I suppose I was in some such mood when in 1973, I became interested in co-forming that year the Irish Labour History Society.

These activities outside whatever trade union work I have done I will regard as having been worthwhile. Of the trade union work, whatever value may be put on the activities in the field of collective bargaining, I will regard as having been worthwhile some of the associated educational and cultural work. I believe a well- justified promotion was that of the Dublin Bakery School. Originally started in a mews at the back of the union premises in Lower Gardiner Street, Dublin, it is now in all but name a national bakery college with a staff of upwards of a dozen teachers.

I regard also the cultural activities with which I was associated in the union as having been important and perhaps, coming near the end of this account, it may be appropriate to cite here one of the songs, of which I wrote the words and music, that our union choir used to sing.

SONG AT PARTING - When Friends Have Met

Too soon the hap - py hours must end. 'Tis
time to part. So let each friend Re - new our
vows to cher - ish dear The ties, the friend - ships
kind-led here.

CHORUS

When friends have met, say not in vain The
hap - py hours have sped a - gain. The song, the
toast, the laugh, the sigh - We'll keep them warm in
mem - or - ry.

2
Like flowers that leave their rich perfume
To wake sweet thought of summer's bloom,
These happy hours, though they be gone,
Their fragrant charm shall linger on.

Chorus

3
This beaker, then, with which we toast
Our parting vows, 'twill hold the most:
For 'tis the heart; in it shall dwell
Each scene, each sound remembered well.

Chorus

I cannot close this account of what may be called my labour history without
some reference to more personal or private matters. I had not begun leading
what I would have regarded as a settled life until 1936, when I was elected a

whole-time official of the union. Even then there were circumstances which made it uncertain that I would be left long in that position. Even the work itself was of a nomadic character. I had to pay periodic visits to the union's branches, and these were located in many parts of the country. In the course of the several years of this itinerant work I changed my domicile a few times. Therefore, I felt little disposed over most of this period to enter into any kind of constant or durable relations with a member of the opposite sex.

Of course over the period I had what may be called liaisons of a more or less social kind with members of the opposite sex, usually ended from incompatibility in politics or religious or other matters. It wasn't until 1940, when I met Harriet Hendy, that I began to feel some of the assurance I thought desirable for permanence with a partner.

Harriet was from a farming family in County Kildare, and at the time was working as a medical nurse in Dublin. Our first meeting was quite fortuitous. I was boarding in the home of a friend of mine, Michael Conroy, in the Donnycarney suburb of the city. The house, but a few years built, was in the larger council-house style, with a small garden area both at the front and the rear of the premises. When it came spring that year there was talk in the house of making a rockery in the front area, along the border of path extending from the street gate to the hall-door of the house.

It was the first of April, and I had been given a few days off from duties in the union. I undertook some of the work on the proposed rockery, and that morning with a canvas sack I betook myself to the seaside resort of Howth, to procure some stones, hopefully sea encrusted, as a basis for the rockery. After some search on the shore and securing some stones that I could manage to carry in the sack to the bus for delivery in Donnycarney, I decided to rest a bit in a café near the sea-front. On my way to the café I saw this young woman, accompanied by a female companion, going in the same direction, and when settled at neighbouring tables in the small café, we casually got into conversation.

This was soon to be followed by meetings with Harriet in the city and our eventual marriage the following year. The marriage, which has given us three children, has endured over the years, and in the year of writing this account moves to its forty-eighth anniversary. I have thought to commit to verse the circumstances narrated above.

HARRIET

> I went to Howth to look for stones
> To border lawn with rockery,
> And flowers to bloom in varied tones,
> And tendriled stems in filigree.
>
> One seldom knows what fate intends,
> Or fathoms what its signs foretell.
> I went to Howth to look for stones,
> And I found there a jewel as well.

A jewel that no jeweller stocked
Or goldsmith ever planned to lay
Or set on monarch royally frocked
For show on Coronation day.

The stones would make a rockery
Of April flowers and tendrils fair.
In Howth what need for such could be
The day that I met Harriet there?

Those stones in Howth had pressed their weight
On clumped sea-weed that there abides.
The shore's sand lipped, as if to sate
The coquetry of ardent tides.

Fine stones have gone in monuments
To famous men and women too,
In flattering sculpture and descants
That often much on fancy drew.

But fancy scarce would be excess
That gilded path where Harriet walked;
And, from her voice's tenderness,
Had deemed it song when 'er she talked.

We saw thin incoming waves caress
Those lips that pouted on the strand.
Or was it waves content to press
Their memorabilia in sand?

For memories oft were better pressed
Where they dissolved without a trace,
With none made sorrow or distressed,
With nought to pardon or efface.

But not our memories of Howth,
We'd wish their spell for aye remet,
As long as tides came in, went out,
And suns and moons did rise and set.

I thus have cited tides and sands,
As having feelings, ev'n of love.
When one's in love its urge expands
Th' imagination's quest or probe.

So 'twas in Howth that April day,
When we first met, our fates now joined.
When everything seemed rich and gay
On strand the very shells seemed coined.

The work of minter, who had planned
To make money beautiful, by artifice
Of form enwhorled, its ear attuned
Not to Mammon's but the sea's voice.

If I had gathered stones to build
Not rockery but place to dwell,
I'd want it not, though treasure-filled
Were Harriet not there as well.

Her graceful form had caught my gaze,
Her artless smile had cast its spell,
Her eyes that their look could eyelids raise
And heart-beats too, p'rh'ps hopes as well.

Those stones from Howth for me remained
As treasure trove that stirred me more
That flowers 'er did that round them twined
But other stones more hallowed were.

If I were one of churchman's faith
In holy form'laries and lauds,
I'd bless the stones that made the path
That led me to where Harriet was.

A path that would our fates entwine
In loving union, and secure
Us love of offspring - p'rh-'ps more fine
Than love of one another, and more pure.

Index